The Navajos

Oscar H. Lipps

**Expand your knowledge.
Increase your power.**

BCR's Shelf2Life program grew from a strong desire to help libraries share their vital collections with new audiences. BCR is the nation's oldest and most established library network, and their mission is to bring libraries together for greater success by expanding their knowledge, reach and power. By helping libraries digitize and widen access to their collections, BCR's Shelf2Life program helps libraries increase the visibility, use and recognition of their important collections. In addition, the program is designed to help researchers, collectors and all curious readers by putting these editions within easy reach: in print-on-demand or electronic format.

Drake University's Cowles Library supports the university's education goals by providing services, collections, technology and learning opportunities that make it possible for faculty and students to successfully access and use information. In fulfilling this mission, the Library works in partnership with faculty and other members of the Drake community and seeks to contribute to the overall goals of the University. Primary emphasis is placed upon materials and services that expand upon and support the curriculum and also support faculty/student research. Expanding electronic access to the Library's rarely accessed historical items will enrich and extend the Library's collections, serving to enhance the development of each student's 'historical consciousness' as well as encouraging collaboration with faculty from disciplines outside the Library. The participation of Drake University in BCR's Shelf2Life program reaffirms the Library's centrality to the learning enterprise and promotes the aims of information literacy, providing faculty, staff, students and researchers with new methods of accessing important content.

Little Histories of North American Indians

THE NAVAJOS

BY
OSCAR H. LIPPS

CEDAR RAPIDS, IOWA
THE TORCH PRESS
:: :: :: 1909 :: :: ::

FOREWORD

Little Histories of North American Indians is designed to give in plain and simple form a concise and authentic history of the North American Indians by tribes. So far, most of the literature giving reliable accounts of the life, manners, customs, habits, religion, mythology, arts, and crafts of the various Indian tribes of our country is contained chiefly in government reports and in scientific works which are either not readily accessible to the reading public, or are too scientific and technical to be enjoyable and entertaining to the average general reader. The aim, then, is a popular and reliable little history of our North American Indians which will, in a measure, satisfy the ever increasing desire on the part of Americans for a more intimate knowledge of the "first of all Americans."

It has not been the intention to present in this little book — the first of the series — any new facts concerning the Navajos, but rather to bring together the facts already known of the tribe.

While not intended as a contribution to ethnological or anthropological science, still it has been the constant aim of the author to confine his statements to the facts, and to this end no pains have been spared in consulting acknowledged authorities on the subject, all of which have been given credit throughout the pages of the book.

O. H. L.

Nez Perces Indian Agency
   Fort Lapwai, Idaho
      September 21, 1908

Washington, Oct. 1, 1908.

My dear Mr. Lipps:

I am more than pleased at what you tell me of the design of your booklet on the Navajos — your hope that it might result in drawing from other writers similar little books on different Indian tribes. They would make a collection of value to that part of the public who take an interest in the history of our aborigines without having the time at command to study the more elaborate and ambitious works on the subject.

Hoping with you that your essay may prove only the first of a series, I am

Sincerely yours,

FRANCIS E. LEUPP.

CONTENTS

APPENDIX

LIST OF ILLUSTRATIONS

A LITTLE HISTORY OF THE NAVAJOS

CHAPTER I

Their Discovery

From the accession of the house of Tras-
tamara, about the middle of the fourteenth cen-
tury, Spain dates the rise of
Westward the her greatness as a world pow-
Course of Conquest er. In the tenth and eleventh
takes its Way centuries the Mohammedans
flourished and prospered in
the southern part of the peninsula, and the Moorish
kingdom of Granada bore witness to a civilization
far more brilliant and splendid than Christian Spain
had hitherto been able to present. Here the lamps
of learning were kept burning while all the rest of
western Europe groped in darkness, and here the
Arabian philosophers had transplanted the sciences
of the East from whence they found their way beyond the Pyrenees and the Rhine, and penetrated the land of the Anglo-Saxons across the
English Channel. Meanwhile, Spain had accom-
plished little that goes to make a wise and powerful
nation.

However, in the course of events, Spain evolved
into a nation. In the year 1469 Aragon and Castile
were united in one kingdom by the marriage of

Ferdinand, surnamed the Catholic, and Isabella. Ferdinand, while possessing ability, was both a bigot and a despot; Isabella was his faithful consort. His overbearing spirit and intolerant mind found fitting expression in the cruel deeds of the bloody Inquisition. His bitter persecution of the Jews was no less cruel and unrelenting than was his hatred for the Moors and heretics. The meek and unoffending Israelites were banished to the number of hundreds of thousands, and their property confiscated. Naked and utterly helpless, they submissively turned their faces to other countries, seeking refuge in Portugal, France, Italy, and the East. This act was a great blow to the future affluence of Spain. The boomerang returned to paralyze the hand that sent it. The nation's life blood had been drained out. Thrifty enterprise waned and the life of trade withered and died. The springs of the nation's commerce, being thus deprived of their source, ran putrid for a while, then dried up altogether. The Moorish Granada was also taken by the Christians and three millions of her people fled to Africa and the East. The hope of the nation had departed — both glory and gold had vanished. New worlds must now be conquered and new sources of revenue added to her possessions.

Christopher Columbus now arrived upon the scene, discovered a new world and thus saved the day for Spain. The hope of the nation lay beyond the Atlantic. Turning her eyes to the West, with sword in one hand and crucifix in the other,

A Navajo Patriarch

she bid priest and soldier embark for the New
World. Knighthood was in flower and the spirit
of conquest the all-absorbing passion — the seeking
of gold and the saving of souls the objects of
adventure.

And lo! westward the course of Spanish conquest took its way.

In 1493, the year after the discovery of the
New World, Pope Alexander VI issued his famous
Bull of Demarcation, in which
Spanish explorers he gave to Spain all that por-
discover the Indians tion of undiscovered country
of the Southwest lying beyond an imaginary
line one hundred miles west
of the Azores and the Cape Verde Islands. Upon
this Spain based her claims to the New World.

Not until 1513 did European explorers venture
into the interior of North America. Previous to this
time they had merely touched upon the shores of the
great western continent. The great beyond appeared
to them dark, void, and impenetrable. Balboa in that
year crossed the Isthmus of Panama, and six years
later Cortez landed on the east coast of Mexico.

The same year that Cortez set out to explore
Mexico (1519), Pineda, another Spanish explorer,
sailed through the Gulf of Mexico, skirting the
shores of the continent from Florida to the province
of Mexico. He soon returned to Spain, giving glowing
accounts of all he had seen. He told DeNarvaez about
the natives he had found in the lower Mississippi

valley; how gaudily they were attired; how 'rich they were in gold and precious gems. Excited by these alluring descriptions of the Mississippi Indians and their brilliant golden ornaments, DeNarvaez set out in 1528 with an expedition to explore and conquer that portion of the country lying to the north and west of the Gulf of Mexico.

He passed through Louisiana and Texas and wandered westward, crossing the Rio Grande, passing through Chihuahua and Sonora, and arriving at Culiacan, through which he passed, reaching the west coast in 1536. When he returned to Spain his account of the wonderful country over which he had traveled, and of the more wonderful people he had encountered on the way, aroused a keen desire in the adventurous Spaniards to make more thorough explorations. They believed that somewhere in this wonderful country would be found the Fountain of Youth, and what was still more to be desired, the fabled Seven Cities which they believed to contain vast stores of piled-up wealth.

One of the Indian tribes of the Southwest had preserved a story of Seven Caves in which they said their ancestors once lived long years before, and the Spaniards thought these to be the legendary Seven Cities. Believing them to be located somewhere to the north, the Spanish governor of Mexico, Mendoza, sent forth Fray Marcos, a Catholic monk, with a few followers in search of them. He passed, en route, through a number of Indian villages, in each of which he was directed to the north. He arrived at last in sight of the pueblo village of Zuni, New Mexico, located about forty miles south of the present town of Gallup, and still the home of the Zuni Indians. There were at this time, it is said, seven of these pueblos comprising the village, all of which were inhabited. Advance guards were sent forward on a reconnoitering expedition to meet the chief of the tribe and announce the arrival of the exploring party. They never returned and it is supposed they were killed by the Indians. Fray Marcos became greatly frightened at this unkindly reception and hurriedly returned to Mexico, having only viewed the Zuni pueblos from a distance. He understood the name of the city he had discovered to be Cibola, and he called these seven Zuni pueblos the Seven Cities of Cibola.

An ancient Spanish legend relates that many years ago when the Arabs overran the Spanish peninsula and took captive the town of Lisbon, a certain priest of that town fled with many followers to a group of islands located somewhere in the Sea of Darkness where he founded seven cities. These cities, so the legend relates, contained hidden treasures of untold wealth. If they might only find the fabled stream to drink from which meant life and love and youth and beauty, and then discover these hidden cities of stored-up wealth, their happiness would be complete and the millennium be at hand.

In 1540, the year following the return of Fray Marcos to Mexico, Francisco de Coronado marched against the Zuni Indians with three hundred soldiers and eight hundred Mexican Indians. On arriving at Zuni he discovered that Fray Marcos had seen only an Indian village and not the fabled Seven Cities. From Zuni Coronado sent Pedro de Tobar, Juan de Padilla and about twenty men to discover Tusayan (Moqui). On their way thither they passed through the country of the Navajo Indians. They visited the Hopi villages of Oraibi and Walpi and there heard about a great river beyond. Returning to Zuni they reported this to Coronado who immediately sent out Lopez de Cardenas with twelve men to find this river. And thus was discovered the Grand Canyon of the Colorado.

And from this also comes our first knowledge of the Navajos.

CHAPTER II

Their Country

What variegated and wonderful formations we encounter in traveling one hundred miles overland **A Desert Country** across this rugged, ragged, desert country! The whole landscape presents a spectacle of deep sepulchral gloom. Old ocean beds, piled-up debris of volcanic eruptions and the remains of pre-historic ages are everywhere to be seen.

If what geologists tell us of the formation of the earth be true — that the vast mountains of piled-up strata are of sedimentary formation — then the process of infiltration through which these immense piles of stone have gone in forming, must have required ages of time.

Something over 5,000 years ago we find the Chaldean monarchy at the height of its affluence and power. The great level plain between the Tigris and the Euphrates rivers was interlaced with a net-work of irrigating canals, and the luxuriant growth of grain and vegetation in this great alluvial valley excited the wonder and admiration of the Greeks so that the historian, Herodotus, like our own Horace Greeley when writing about the large trees of California, would not tell the whole truth for fear his veracity might be doubted. The Assyrian and Baby-

lonian empires successively rose and fell in the land
of the ancient Chaldeans, and the country where the
hanging gardens of Babylon once spread their rich
perfumes over a land of emerald green, to-day presents a scene as ruined and desolate as that of our own
dry, sand-choked desert of the great Southwest.

To the speculative mind the comparison might
suggest the possibility of a time, in years vastly remote, when this old dry desert of Navajo land presented a very different appearance, and supported a
population well advanced in the arts and sciences of
civilization.

Situated in the northeastern portion of Arizona
and in the northwestern part of New Mexico is the
Navajo reservation, now the larg-
Their Reservation est Indian reservation in the
United States, comprising as
it does nearly ten million acres, or nearly fifteen
thousand square miles, being equal in size to the
combined areas of Massachusetts, Connecticut, and
Rhode Island.

The home of the Navajo Indian has always been
considered one of the most arid and barren portions
of the Great American Desert. The average rainfall
in this region is from ten to fourteen inches, and
is usually confined to two short seasons. The valleys
and lower levels are destitute of trees, save for the
cottonwoods that fringe the banks of the arroyas and
running streams, though the mesas and mountains are
fairly well covered with pinyon, cedar, oak, juniper,

white pine, and spruce. The elevation is from four to
ten thousand feet above sea level, with an attendant
climate unsuited to the luxuriant growth of vegetation. The yucca, cactus, sage brush, gramma grass,
and a few weeds and wild flowers are to be found in the
valleys and on the lower plateaus, while much of the
country is a barren waste with few running streams
or springs and with little else to invite either man or
beast.

The country is extremely diversified in character,
consisting as it does of broad valleys and rolling prai-
ries in the northern and western portions along the
San Juan and Colorado rivers, while the eastern and
southeastern portions are greatly broken by deep canyons, towering mountains, elevated table lands, and
irregular, broken valleys. Vast strata of bituminous
coal extend north and south through almost the entire
length of the reservation, some veins being thirty
feet in thickness. No precious metals or other minerals of value have ever been discovered in this territory.

Owing to the high altitude, the winters are long
and cold and the season for growing and maturing
crops is correspondingly short. A little corn, wheat,
oats and alfalfa, and a variety of vegetables are grown
in the valleys where water can be had for irrigating.
In many of the valleys fruit culture can be carried
on with profit, but since his peach orchards were
laid waste by the soldiers forty years ago, the Navajo
has paid little or no attention to the growing of fruit.

His staple agricultural product is Indian corn. If he can only raise a crop of corn his sustenance is assured for the year.

Although a sun-burnt desert of sand, sage brush, cactus, and piled-up debris of great volcanic eruptions, the Navajo country is a land of enchantment. Here Nature seems to have forgotten her modesty and laid bare to vulgar gaze the inmost recesses of her anatomy. Her very vitals, loose and dismembered, lie in massive, mournful state where they were expelled centuries ago by the mighty power of some pent-up energy or internal strife. Vast beds of lava and masses of melted rock and minerals lie everywhere in huge mountains. The traveler in Navajo land, gazing on the form of a world in the making, finds himself transported to another planet, as it were, ere he is aware. Here he sees written, as if by the fingers of Divinity, the story of the creation; and as he views the mighty, massive, wonderfully illustrated and awe-inspiring pages of Nature's book, as it lies opened before his vision, he sees not God in burning bush, but rather meets him face to face.

The white man is out of place in this veritable holy of holies. Unlike the native red man he does not adorn and beautify the nude landscape. At the approaching footsteps of civilization Nature seems to seek seclusion in the pavilion of her own magnificent mazes, and to reserve her beauty and her smiles for her own children and sympathetic worshipers. And if it be true that man is happy in proportion as he is in harmony with his sur-

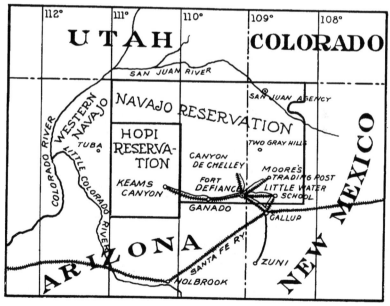

Map of Navajo Reservation

roundings, then the Navajo Indian is truly a
happy being. In his daily life he unconscious-
ly fulfils the injunction uttered by Aristotle
more than two thousand years ago when he said,
"Know the world of nature of which you are a part,
and you will be yourself and know yourself without
thought or effort. The things you see you are."

Listen to this beautiful description of a summer
day in Navajo land by Mr. U. S. Hollister, as given
in his book, *The Navajo and His Blanket*:

Slowly the darkness of early morn falls back
before the shafts of a rising sun. The keen arrows
of light pierce its mantle, and it
A Summer Day in   is driven fleeting to the west.
Navajo Land   The sun is master; his morning
rays dry the earth. The vapor
rises from the streams in the valley, at first in little
threads of white, like smoke from a dying campfire;
then gathering volume, it ascends until the course of
the stream is plainly marked by a pearly white
drapery that curtains the brightness of the new-born
day. Lazily expanding, and growing darker, the mist
assumes the form of threatening clouds, and these float
up the canyons and brush against the mountain sides,
spraying the verdure with diamonds of dew, and baptizing it in the name of the glorious Orb of Day, — the
Indian's Father of All. Then they whiten again as
they are bleached by the sun, and, stirred by the
breeze, go tumbling over the mountains like great
fleecy sheep at play. Beautiful in contrast with the
purple haze of the ranges, the azure of the sky, and
the light of the morning, yet they soon separate into
slender strands of mist which wander off into space
and are lost.

And now everything is bathed in sunshine. The snow glistens on the peaks; the odor of pine and of cedar fills the air; the pure ozone tempts the lungs to full expansion. The world of wilderness is awake. And this is Morning in Navajo land.

As the noontime approaches, the sun seems to pause overhead, when, in a dome of purest blue, it glows and burns and parches the earth; but under its influence, the valleys have revealed their wealth of wild flowers, cactus, sage and bright leafed shrubs that rival the barbaric colors of oriental drapery. The mountains, with their gleaming caps of snow, stand out in strong relief, in blue and gray and purple tints, and in ever shifting lights and shadows. An eagle, slowly and in great circles, soars high in the blue sky. A coyote calls to his mate across the miles between mesa and mesa, or, in shade of cedar, idles or naps the day away — lazy vagabond waiting for the night. On a distant trail, a Navajo on horse-back, watching his sheep, shades his eyes and looks across the valley into the vast expanse of light, and in the distance he can see the smoke from the hut he calls home. He looks at the grandeur of the whole scene through the rarefied air of an elevation of more than a mile above the sea, through an atmosphere which, acting like the lense of a telescope, brings far distant objects within easy range. The great panorama of mountain and plain, of mesa and valley, of arroya and canyon, shaded here and there by pine and cedar, dwarfs every living thing. The stillness is the stillness of solitude, the beauty, the beauty of Nature undefiled.

And this is Mid-day in Navajo land.

As the afternoon grows old, the glare fades; and the sun, touching the rugged horizon, casts long shadows across the plains; and then like a blazing meteor, drops out of sight behind the snow capped mountains.

Now turn your eyes to the west and look upon the glorious beauty of a sunset in a strange land. The peaks stand out like sentinels guarding the retreat of day, and a blaze of light whitens the sunward side of those to the right and to the left. Fragments of gathering clouds, floating above in a sea of azure in which are blended tints of gray and green and yellow, are rich with the colors of red and gold and scarlet and purple which shift and change before our gaze as the misty masses drift with the evening breeze. Through this wealth of brilliant colors and mingled hues and tints, the sun projects its rays in fan-like form far into space, the shafts and beams of light illuminating the whole, and completing a rare picture of magnificence that inspires feelings of reverence and humility in those who look upon it. You close your eyes and wonder if anything else of this world can be so beautiful. The fiery glory behind the mountains dies down, but twilight lingers long as it slowly yields its beauty to the gathering shades of night.

And this is Evening in Navajo land.

One after another the stars appear; slowly and shyly at first, one here and one there; then springing into myriads all at once. The rising moon is hidden by the mountains, and her soft white light reflected on the clouds that float around and above the peaks, transforms them into masses of white and gold. As we stand in the deep shadow, the mountains are outlined in frosted silver by the light of the moon that we can not see, and with this and the hues of the illuminated clouds before us, the grandly beautiful scene is like the one we associate with the work of enchantment — a most wonderful combination of moonlight effects in the mountain region of Navajo land. As she rises the moon's rim comes into view where two mountains look at each other across a canyon; and peering through this notch in the range, she seems to be asking "Is it night? May I come?" But without awaiting our bidding she presents herself in all her splendor; and the mountains and the cliffs and the villages — all the wide landscape around us, are flooded with her light and do homage to her majesty, the Queen of Night — the Indian's Mother of all Mankind.

The soughing of the pines as they are stirred by the rising breeze, is like the murmur of a distant sea, and warns us that the Storm King has had his battle array of thunder clouds hidden behind the mountains. Now, as he leads them over the range, the wind rustles down the gorges, whirls around the foot-hills, and sweeps across the mesas and through the canyons, raising great billows of dust. "The air is tremulous with the energy of the approaching storm." Suddenly all is quiet; but soon the great rain-drops begin to fall — big warm tears of the clouds. Thicker and faster they come until the land is drenched, and new-made rivers roar in the canyons and flood the arroyas with their turbid waters. The clouds have swept over us, and in the silvery light that fills the night, we watch the retreating storm and hear the distant, sullen thunder that rumbles like the cannonading of a retiring army that has spent its strength. Far away dull flashes of lightning still tell of the storm that is gone; but the moon and the stars seem brighter than before, though low in the east is a touch of the faint first glow that heralds the coming of another day.

And this was a Summer Day in Navajo land.

Reared amid such scenes as these, where all Nature cries aloud in a thousand different voices, and speaks to him in prophetic tongues tuned to the keynote of Divinity, what wonder that the Navajo,

With untutored mind
Sees God in the clouds,
Or hears him in the winds?

And who among us, even in the light of revelation, is prepared to say the Navajo's God is not also our God, and that he worships Him as much in spirit and in truth as do his more enlightened white brothers? In the mere matter of form of worship, may we not ask, which is the savage?

Located about fifty miles north of Fort Defiance, Arizona, is the wonderful canyon de Chelly (pronounced de Shay). Nearly two **Cliff Dwellings and** hundred ruins have been lo-**Ancient Ruins** cated in this canyon, among them some very large villages. Some are located high up in the recesses of the canyon's walls, while others occupy more level and accessible positions at the bottom. This canyon is known as one of the ancient homes of the Cliff Dwellers, and ethnologists have visited it frequently and have made numerous excavations in the hope that discoveries might be made that would throw some light on the remarkable little people who built their homes in the almost inaccessible recesses of deep canyons and precipitous walls.

The general opinion among ethnologists of to-day, however, is not as has generally been supposed, that the Aztecs built these villages, but that they were built by the ancestors of the present Pueblo Indians. In fact there is much to lead one to conclude that their assumption is justified by the evidence. In this region the air is so dry and the atmosphere so pure, that articles buried in the ground will continue in a state of preservation for a remarkably long time. In some of these ancient ruins have been found rooms arranged very much like a Pueblo house of the present day. Many objects of every day use in present day pueblos, such as the mealing stone, earthen vessels, ornaments, garments, etc., have been found in these old ruins. Tons of pottery, similar to that made at the present time by the Pueblo Indians, have been unearthed; also in the graves or burial cysts have been found cotton cloth, sandals, and various ceremonial articles, similar to those now in common use among these Indians. With the hundreds of such specimens that have been found and carefully preserved, it is possible to reconstruct the rooms of many of the old cliff dwellings and ancient ruins so that almost any Pueblo Indian would even in this day and time feel himself quite at home within the ancient walls of the house of his ancestors, who were doubtless its inmates perhaps thousands of years ago.

In western New Mexico, sixty-five miles north of the Santa Fé railroad, in Chaco Canyon, is the famous Pueblo Bonito. This is an ancient ruin and was partly explored by the Hyde Exploring Expedition under the direction of Dr. George H. Pepper, the work being carried on for the American Museum of Natural History. This pueblo contains some five hundred rooms with massive outer walls. These ruins are about five hundred feet long and three hundred feet wide. Over fifty thousand genuine turquoise beads, pendants and ornaments of very great value were found in one of the rooms of this pueblo.

This ruin, and such ruins as those which are to be found scattered over the Navajo country, have been accepted by some as evidences that the land now occupied by the Navajos was once peopled by a race concerning whom the Navajos have, according to Dr. Pepper, both myths and traditions; a people, perhaps, more skilled in the arts of peace and war than were any of the other Indian tribes of the Southwest before the advent of the white man.

Such, then, is Navajo land. A desert "land of little rain; of canyon-rift and cactus-plain."

CHAPTER III

The People

Little is definitely known of the early history of the Navajo. By language he is closely related to the Apaches and to the many other **Early History** tribes speaking the Athapascan tongue. He has a faint tradition of a home farther to the north, but whence or when he came to his present abode he has no definite knowledge or tradition.

The word "Navajo" is of Spanish origin, and is said by some to have been applied by the Spanish invaders to that portion of country lying along, and contingent to, the Little Colorado and San Juan rivers. The Spaniards called the inhabitants of that region "Apaches de Navajoa," probably from their resemblance to the Apaches with whom they had previously come in contact. They never refer to themselves as Navajos except when in conversation with white people. They call themselves "Dene," or "Tinneh" — meaning "the people," and they believe themselves to be far superior in every way to any other tribe of Indians.

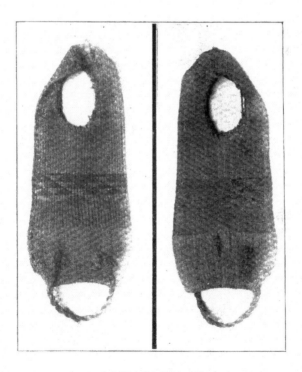

Cliff Dwellers' Sandals
More than 1000 Years Old
(From Photo by Hollister)

There is abundant testimony in the numerous well preserved ruins, that years before the Navajo came to his present home, a pre-**Evidence of a** historic people, advanced in the **Pre-historic Race** ways of civilization, dwelt in this region. The remains of ancient irrigating canals and reservoirs furnish evidence that a people once tilled the soil when natural conditions were different from what we now find them in the Navajo country. Remains of buildings are yet to be seen there of such design and proportions as would indicate the previous presence of a people skilled in architecture and engineering. Archaeologists differ as to the conclusions to be drawn from the evidence contained in these vast ruins. Some are of the opinion that the ancestors of the present Pueblo Indians were the builders of structures such as the one recently uncovered at Pueblo Bonito, New Mexico. Others contend that a race of people far superior in mental and physical endowments must have once lived and labored where now the Navajo leads his peaceful flocks in quiet solitude over a ruined and desolate waste. While it is doubtful if we shall ever know the exact truth as to the history of the people who have so indelibly left their imprint on the desert wastes, still to many it will ever be a pleasant occupation to speculate as to the probable condition of those people who, for aught we know, may have been prouder than the grandees of Spain and more chivalrous in love and war than the plumed knights of early

England. And who knows but they may yet be the theme that in some future day will inspire a Homer or incite a Virgil to sing in deathless song the glories of another and more illustrious Ilium or the prowess and adventure of other and more renowned Trojans?

It is generally supposed that in very early times the Navajos were wild, reckless, roaming Indians without any definite or limited territory they called their home. Unlike most other Indian tribes, there appears to be no fixed, or even prevailing, Navajo type. They vary in feature and stature, from the tall, lithe men with prominent features resembling the Sioux or Cheyennes, to the dwarfish, timid physiognomy of the effeminate Pueblos, with almost every variety between these extremes. The Navajo is thought to have been a general outlaw, roaming at will wherever his fancy or love for adventure might lead him, seeking at all times what or whom he might devour. He continually waged war upon the more peaceful and sedentary Pueblos and gradually gathered to himself the lawless and outcasts of other tribes with whom he frequently came in contact. These in time he assimilated, almost completely changing his character, until to-day, after being subjugated, tamed and disciplined by United States soldiers, we find him peace-loving and industrious, pursuing the quiet industries of agriculture and stock-raising. For three hundred years or more, he has occupied his present country, living much the same to-day as he did three centuries ago. His characteristics and racial instincts are as marked in him today as when Coronado led the Spanish Invasion into New Mexico in 1540.

The Navajo Indians are wards of the general Government under the Department of the Interior.

Government The Navajo reservation is divided into districts which are under the supervision of Indian Superintendents, with headquarters at Fort Defiance, Tuba, Leupp and Keam's Canyon, Arizona, and Shiprock, New Mexico, who have general oversight over them, and who, with Indian police, preserve law and order on the reservation under rules prescribed by the Commissioner of Indian Affairs.

The Navajos have no head chief, but they have a number of "head-men" whom they recognize as leaders, generally because of their superior qualities, character and integrity. While these offices are often either elective or hereditary, still they are not always so. The office of "head-man" usually gravitates to the man who can hold it — a natural born leader of men.

The tribe is composed of several gentes or clans, each clan having its leader, or head-man. The legends of the Navajos contain many accounts of other Indians being adopted into the tribe and intermarrying among them and forming new gentes. The following legendary account of how the Navajos were once joined by a large band of Indians and how they were adopted into the tribe is taken from Dr. Washington Matthews's *Navajo Legends*:

They were joined on the San Juan by a numerous band who came originally from a place called Thapaha-kal-kai (White Valley among the Waters), which is where the city of Santa Fé now stands. These people had long viewed in the western distance the mountains where the Navajos dwelt, wondering if anyone lived there, and at length decided to go thither. They journeyed westward twelve days till they reached the mountains, and they spent eight days travelling among them before they encountered the Navajos. Then they settled at Toindotsos (place) and lived there twelve years, subsisting on ducks and fish, but making no farms. All this time they were friendly to the Navajos and exchanged visits; but, finding no special evidence of relationship with the latter, they dwelt apart. When at length they came to the San Juan to live, marriages had taken place between the two tribes, and the people from Among the Waters became a part of the Navajo nation, forming the gens THA-PA-HA. They lived at a place called Hyietyin (Trails Leading Upward), close to the Navajos. There was a smooth sandy plain, which they thought would be good for farming, and the Chief, whose name was Gontso, or Big Knee, had stakes set around the plain to show that his people claimed it. The people of the new gens were good hunters, skilled in making weapons and beautiful buck-skin shirts, and they taught their art to the other gentes.

The Tha-pa-ha then spoke a language more like the modern Navajo than that which the other gentes spoke. The languages were not alike. The chief of the Tsin-ad-zi-ni and Gontso often visited one another at night, year after year, for the purpose of uniting the two languages and picking out the words in each that were best. But the words of the Tha-pa-ha were usually the best and plainest; so the new language resembles the Tha-pa-ha more than it resembles the Old Navajo.

While the Tha-pa-ha lived at Hyietyin they had always abundant crops, — better crops than their neighbors had, sometimes they could not harvest all they raised, and let food lie ungathered in the field. They built stone store-houses, something like pueblo houses, among the cliffs, and in these stored their corn. The store houses stand there yet. The Tha-pa-ha remained at Hyietyin thirteen years, during which time many important events occurred, and then they moved to Azdeltsigi.

Gontso had twelve wives; four of these were from the gens of Tsinadzini, four from the gens of Dsiltlani, and four from the gens of Thanezani. He used to give much grain from his abundant harvests to the gentes to which his wives belonged; but, in spite of his generosity, his wives were unfaithful to him. He complained to their relations and to their chiefs, these remonstrated with the wives, but failed to improve their ways. At last they lost patience with the women and said to Gontso; "Do with them as you will. We will not interfere." So the next wife whom he detected in crime, he mutilated in a shameful way, and she died in consequence. He cut off the ears of the next transgressor, and she, too, died. He amputated the breasts of the third wife who offended him, and she died also. He cut off the nose of the fourth; she did not die. He determined then that cutting off the nose should, in future, be the greatest punishment imposed on the faithless wife, — something that would disfigure but not kill, — and the rest of the people agreed with him. But this had no effect on the remaining wives; they continued to lapse from virtue till all were noseless. Then they got together and began to plot mischief against their husband, Big Knee. They spoke so openly of their evil intentions that he feared to let any of them stay in the lodge at night and he slept alone.

About this time the people determined to have a great ceremony for the benefit of Big Knee; so they made great preparations and held a rite of nine days duration. During its progress the mutilated women remained in a hut by themselves, and talked about the unkindness of their people and the vengeance due to their husband. They said one to another: "We should leave our people and go elsewhere." On the last night of the ceremony there was a series of public exhibitions in a corral, or circle of branches, such as the Navajos have now on the last night in the ceremony of the mountain chant, and among the different *alili*, or entertainments of the night, was a dance by the mutilated women. When their time came they entered the circle, each bearing a knife in her hand, and danced around the central fire, peering among the spectators as if searching for their husband; but he was hidden in the wall of branches that formed the circle. As they danced they sang a song the burden of which was "Pesla asila" (It was the knife that did it to me). When they had finished their dance they left the corral and, in the darkness without, screamed maledictions at their people, saying; "May the waters drown ye! May the winters freeze ye! May the fires burn ye! May the lightnings strike ye!" and much more. Having cursed till they were tired, they departed for the far north, where they still dwell, and now, whenever they turn their faces to the south, we have cold winds and storms and lightning.

The Navajos perpetuate these legends as nearly as is possible by a people having no written language, in the pristine purity of their fore-fathers; and while the federal authority extends over the reservation and punishes infractions of the law, the Navajos have a code of honor and morals handed down from generation to generation since they first became a nation, and they have ever regarded it as their sacred duty to obey this code under penalty of ostracism, death, or banishment from the tribe.

CHAPTER IV
Their Manners and Customs

The coming of the Spaniard wrought a great change in the life and occupation of the Navajos.

A Pastoral People It is related that long ago, soon after the Spaniards migrated with their flocks to the country of the Navajos, a marauding party of these Indians were out on a foraging expedition in the vicinity of the Rio Grande River and by stealth secured a small flock of sheep and goats from a Spanish settlement and took them home with them. These animals so delighted the women and children of the tribe that no pains were spared to bestow upon them the tenderest care and greatest consideration. The Navajos soon proved to be exceptionally good shepherds and under their care the flocks increased rapidly and a great deal of attention has ever since been given by them to the raising of sheep. The flocks are tended almost entirely by the women and children, Navajo women being, perhaps, the best shepherds in the world. They watch over their flocks as tenderly as a mother watches over her infant child. When the weather is cold and damp they frequently take the little lambs into their hogans and wrap them up in soft, woolly skins to protect them from the chilling blasts, and should a young lamb lose its mother the Navajo woman will

A Cliff Dwelling

(From the *Southern Workman*)

often nurse it from her own breast as she would her infant.

Being preëminently a pastoral people, there can scarcely be found a Navajo family on the reservation that does not possess a flock of sheep and goats, ranging in numbers from a few hundred to several thousand head. It is no uncommon sight to see two or three small children watching their herds far out on the desert waste or mountain side with no other company than their flock, their faithful dogs and the ever present Mexican burro, whose voices are the only sounds that have disturbed the solemn stillness which has hung over many remote places in this strange land since creation.

And so we to-day find the Navajo Indians the greatest aboriginal pastoral people in the New World.

The Navajo Indian can hardly be said to have a permanent home. He is a wanderer over a desert land, roaming at will from place to place with his flocks and herds in summer, and in winter seeking shelter sometimes in the foothills, but often high up on the mountain sides, where he can secure fuel for the rudely constructed hogan he calls his home. That he enjoys his domestic fireside there can be no doubt, since he lives contented and happy, ever increasing and multiplying.

Their Home

In his domestic life he practices a code of morals after which many of his more enlightened white brothers would do well to pattern. **Their Domestic Life** The Navajo father is kind to his wife and children and in return they practice uniform obedience to him. The Navajo child is seldom punished and never beaten, for the simple reason that he seldom requires it. There appears to be a bond of sympathy and love between parent and child which is very strong during the minority of the child but strange to say, the children do not always love and protect their parents when the latter become old and infirm. To them the very old and decrepit have few rights which they are bound to respect.

The women are generally virtuous, the "perverse woman" being an object of universal scorn. The Navajos believe her to be the very incarnation of the *chindee* (evil spirit), and that at death her spirit enters a fish. Hence the Navajo's utter horror and hatred of the finny tribe.

It is a maxim of the tribe that a Navajo has the right to have as many wives as he can pay for and support. He secures his wives by pur- **Marriage** chase and the Navajo maiden is never lacking in offers of marriage. However, she is not at liberty to choose her own husband, but is rather a standing invitation of her mother for as many informal proposals as she may be able to attract, with the understanding that the mother re-

serves the right to reject any and all bids if deemed
for the best interests of her own exchequer. The
daughters are the property of the mothers until mar-
ried, then both the daughter and her husband belong
to the mother. Custom requires that the man must never, under penalty of some awful calamity befalling the
whole family, look his mother-in-law in the face.

Because the young women command high
prices, often beyond the amount the young man
is able to pay, as a rule the old men marry the young
girls and the young men frequently marry old women.
After they have made their fortune they may then
marry young women. It requires several ponies and
a good flock of sheep to buy a young and buxom
Navajo maiden. At death all the property of the
husband descends not to the wife and children, but to
the brothers and distant relatives of the husband.

The Navajos still preserve their old Indian marriage customs. Their marriage ceremony is one of the
most beautiful of any of
The Wedding Ceremony   the tribes. It is thus des-
cribed by Mr. A. M. Stev-
ens:

On the night set for the wedding both families
and their friends meet at the hut of the bride's family.
Here there is much feasting and singing, and the
bride's family makes return presents to the bridegroom's people, but not, of course, to the same amount.
The women of the bride's family prepare corn meal
porridge, which is poured into the wedding basket.
The bride's uncle then sprinkles a circular ring and

cross of the sacred blue pollen of the lark spur upon the porridge, near the outer edge and in the center.

The bride has hitherto been lying beside her mother, concealed under a blanket, on the woman's side of the hogan (hut). After calling to her to come to him, her uncle seats her on the west side of the hut, and the bridegroom sits down before her, with his face toward her's and the basket of porridge set between them. A gourd of water is then given to the bride, who pours some of it on the bridegroom's hands while he washes them, and he then performs a like office for her. With the first two fingers of the right hand he then takes a pinch of porridge, just where the line of pollen touches the circle of the east side. he eats this one pinch, and the bride dips with her finger from the same place. He then takes in succession a pinch from the other places where the lines touch the circle and a final pinch from the center, the bride's fingers following his. The basket of porridge is then passed over to the younger guests, who speedily devour it with merry clamor, a custom analogous to dividing the bride's cake at a wedding. The elder relatives of the couple now give them much good and weighty advice, and the marriage is complete.

The Navajo in his plural marriages often has among his wives the mother and her daughter by a previous husband. Should he marry an old woman who has a young daughter, it is not an uncommon practice for the Navajo to marry this daughter when she arrives at the age of nubility and in so doing he prevents the mother-in-law hoodoo and becomes his own father-in-law by adoption.

Marriage among the Navajos is quite frequently a probational alliance, about one year elapsing before they publicly acknowledge their matrimonial relationship. When the young man marries he loses his identity with his own family and lives with, and becomes a member of, his wife's family and the children, if any, belong to the mother and take the name of her gens. No Navajo can lawfully marry one of his own gens, and they seldom form matrimonial alliances or mix with the white race in any manner. As a result we find the Navajos preserving their old customs, habits and modes of life in much the same undefiled manner to-day as before the white man made his appearance among them.

The Navajo Indians were formerly slave owners. It was their custom to hold as hostages all captives taken in war from other tribes, and these **Slavery** were often held in slavery for the remainder of their lives. While most of their slaves were taken from among the Ute and Piute tribes, still it is said that they also often captured Mexican women and held them in slavery. It is also true that many Mexicans captured Navajo women and sold them into bondage. More than fifteen hundred Navajo slaves were held by the whites and Mexicans of New Mexico and Arizona when the United States acquired that territory from Mexico. It is more than probable that the Navajos got their idea of abject slavery from their experiences with the Mexicans.

The *Shaman* or medicine-man is the high priest of the Navajos. He professes to cure all the ills of mind and body. In fact to the **The Medicine-man** Navajo disease is nothing more than the workings of evil spirits. He believes if this evil spirit can be driven out of his body he will speedily recover. The *Shaman* may often be sincere in his belief that he possesses the power to drive out the evil spirit and thus restore health, but no doubt he more often knows that he possesses no such power but it is to his interest to make the people believe that he possesses it.

In the first place the medicine-man must have visible, optical assurance of his pay or he will refuse to "sing" until it is forthcoming. He is most exacting in his demands for compensation for unless he receive his price in advance his ability to effect a cure is greatly endangered. He is very careful to explain to the patient that if he doesn't exact the fee the gods will get mad at him and will refuse to answer his prayers. This is usually a convincing argument and the fee is forthcoming.

The Navajo leads a strenuous open air life. He possesses great powers of endurance, is active, quick, alert and ever ready **The Discipline of their Life** to strike a bargain whereby he may enrich his coffers. He has never been pauperized by the government and has kept alive his racial instincts and his tribal initiative. Necessity early taught him that much hard labor is required to extract a living from a barren desert and he has not forgotten the lesson. He lives close to nature, wears no hat, does not restrict the free use of his body by the use of suspenders and seldom puts anything into his mouth to steal away his brains. He has his faults, but with all that he keeps his passions well under control. With head high and lungs expanded he goes forth to do whatever his hands find to do and he does not give up. With him work is a matter of necessity, not always of choice, but in his own country, in his own way, and after the manner of his forefathers he is at home, living one day at a time, never borrowing trouble and enjoying the freedom of his own mountain abode.

The Navajos have a great variety of games and sports which they formerly practiced greatly to their amusement and physical well-being.

Games and Sports   A favorite sport among them now in the way of matching physical dexterity and endurance is foot races. There are probably no better runners among any other Indians in the United States especially for long distances. They will often run for several miles at a stretch and a Navajo will take a message across the desert on foot and run a distance of twenty or thirty miles, scarcely stopping. He is fleet of foot but above all is the remarkable power of endurance he displays in making long journeys across the desert and mountains.

The game of Cat's Cradle was once a game much played by the Navajos, and the myth of the game is thus given by Rev. Berard Haile:

Cat's Cradle owes its origin to the spider people. They, the spiders, who in the Navajo belief were human beings, taught them the game for their own amusement. The holy spider taught the Navajo to play and how to make the various figures of stars, snakes, bears, coyottes, etc., but on one condition — they were to play only in winter, because at that season spiders, snakes, etc., sleep and do not see them. To play the Cat's Cradle at any other time of the year would be folly, for certain death by lightning, falling from a horse, or some other mishap were sure to reach the offender. Otherwise no religious meaning is said to attach to the game. Some claim it is to teach the children the location of the stars.

Some of the other games and sports indulged in by the Navajos are similar to those practiced by many other tribes of American Indians, such as archery, hidden ball, dice games, shinny, ball race, etc.

The Navajos do not like to bury their dead themselves though they are always willing the white people should do so for them. Their superstition prevents them from even so much as touching a dead person if possible to prevent doing so. Before life has entirely left the body it is the custom to wrap it in a new blanket and carry it to some convenient secluded spot where it is deposited on top of the ground or beneath some projecting cliff or rock, together with all the personal effects of the deceased. If an infant, the cradle, trinkets, etc.,

The Burial

A Navajo Woman in Native Dress

are carefully deposited beside the body. When there are no longer signs of life stones are piled around and over it, in order, they say, to keep the wolves and coyotes from carrying it away. If the deceased be a grown person the favorite saddle horse is led to the body where it is killed in a most brutal manner by knocking it in the head with axe or club. Here it lies by the form of its late owner, ready for the journey to the great spirit world.

If by chance a Navajo should die suddenly before he can be removed from the hogan, they sometimes ply the firebrand and burn up the hut with all its contents, thus cremating the dead. Believing that the evil spirit enters the form at death and that if they should come in contact with a dead body or were to enter a hogan in which one of their number had died, the evil spirit would enter into them and kill them instantly, they are afraid to touch it or even to enter the hogan in which the person died.

Upon the death of the head of a Navajo family all of his personal property descends to his brothers, sisters, uncles and aunts to the exclusion of his wife and children, a custom which is often very harmful in its effects, since if the wife should happen not to be possessed of some property in her own right she and the children are made to suffer penury and want.

CHAPTER V

Wars and Treaties

Perhaps no other tribe of North American Indians were ever so successful, through so many years, in warfare with the white man as were

As Warriors the Navajos. While history fails to record a single great battle with the Navajos such as our armies have fought with the Sioux, Comanches, Apaches and others, still they carried on a continual desultory warfare with whites, Mexicans and neighboring tribes of Indians for more than one hundred and eighty years, with few intervals of peace. From 1849 to 1867 the United States expended annually over three million dollars in fighting and feeding the Navajos. In fact for many years the Navajos believed themselves the most formidable warriors on the face of the earth. They did not possess the least doubt as to their ability successfully to engage the combined armies of the United States and Mexico with the Utes and Piutes thrown in for good measure. And why not? Did not General Canby, General Garland, General Sumner and many other brave soldiers of our army march into their country bent on exterminating the whole tribe, and then straightway march out again happy in the thought that they had been permitted to escape with their lives? Why then should the Navajo have any

fears? In numbers he believed himself far superior
to the rest of the world. Taking a handful of sand
he would let it slowly dribble through his fingers
upon the ground, and when the last grain had passed
through he would point to the little heap below and
say "White soldiers all the same as the grains in this
little heap of sand." Then turning to the broad expanse of mountain and plain extending for miles
and miles all around him, he would make a low circular sweep and with outstretched arm pointing to the
grass covered mountains, plains and table lands, would
say, "Navajos all the same as the blades of grass."

But the Navajos forgot to reckon with Kit Carson.
"Father Kit," as the Pueblo Indians called him, was
not only a trapper, hunter, guide, sol-
Kit Carson dier, and Indian agent, but he possessed
the capacity, in a marvelous degree, of
making quick decisions at just the right time. The
distinguishing traits of his character were integrity,
bravery, and skilful leadership. The Navajos, when
they once knew Kit, admired him. He always told
them the truth, "talked one way," and so completely
were they surprised and overwhelmed by his shrewd
tactics that one engagement was all that was needed
to convince them that they had better make terms
with Kit at once, and practically the whole tribe surrendered to him with very little bloodshed. They
soon learned that he would punish them if they did
wrong, and that he would also defend them if they
were wronged by the whites.

The last Navajo war was begun in 1861 and ended two or three years later. A negro slave was killed
by the Navajos at Fort De-
The Last Navajo War fiance, Arizona, the slave belonging to one of the army
officers stationed at that post. The military authorities demanded that the murderer be brought in. The Indians refused to comply with the demand. War was declared. The Navajos entered upon a series of hostile incursions into the Mexican settlements, capturing stock and committing other acts of depredation. The governor of the territory was appealed to, and public sentiment generally aroused against the Navajos. A mighty effort was now to be made to annihilate these "butchering Navajos."

In 1862 General Sibley, of the Confederate army, marched into New Mexico from Texas with a force of
armed men and attracted the
General Sibley   attention of the United States
Invades New Mexico troops then stationed in the
Territory. Taking advantage of the situation the Navajos and Apaches began robbing the citizens of their stock and committing other acts of depredation among the white settlements. Henry Connelly, then governor of New Mexico, issued a proclamation directing that the commander-in-chief of the militia reorganize his forces and proceed to subdue and chastise the "perfidious" Navajos.

"For many years past you have been suffering from the hostile inroads of a perfidious tribe of Indians, who, notwithstanding the **The Proclamation** efforts of the government to ameliorate their condition and administer to their wants in every respect, do not cease daily to encroach upon the rights and depredate upon the lives and property of the peaceful citizens of New Mexico.

"For a long series of years have we been subjected to the rapacity and desolation of this hostile tribe, which has reduced many a wealthy citizen to poverty, and the greater part of our citizens to want and mendicacy; which has murdered hundreds of our people, and carried our women and children into captivity. Almost every family in the Territory has to mourn the loss of some loved one who has been made a sacrifice to these bloodthirsty Navajos. Our highways are insecure, and the entire country is now invaded and overrun by these rapacious Indians, murdering, robbing, and carrying off whatever may come in their way. Such a state of things cannot and must not longer be endured.

"For more than a year past we have been menaced by, and finally suffered the invasion of, Texas forces; to repel which, and relieve the Territory from that more powerful and not less rapacious foe, required all the energies and exhausted the resources of the Territory. During this period of time the Indians have, with impunity, preyed upon every interest of our people, and reduced them to a state of poverty which has not been felt for the last fifty years.

"We are now free from all appearance of a confederate force upon our frontier, but the attention of the military will be constantly drawn to any new dangers that may threaten from the same, or any other quarter, and will, consequently, not be able to send into the Indian country any large force for the length of time necessary to subjugate the Indians and recapture the immense amount of property of which our people have been so recently despoiled. This duty pertains to the militia of the Territory; for this purpose you are to organize, never to be disbanded until we have secured indemnity for the past and security for the future.

"It belongs to the people to relieve themselves of the evils they are suffering, and administer such chastisement to these marauders as they deserve. We have power to do so, and that power must be exercised.

"Therefore, I, Henry Connelly, governor of the Territory of New Mexico, and commander-in-chief of the militia forces thereof, do hereby order all the field and staff officers of said forces immediately to proceed to the reorganization of the militia, in conformity with the law in force on the subject, and under such rules and regulations as may be prescribed, and to have said militia ready to march to the Navajo country by the 15th of October next. The adjutant general is hereby ordered to carry this proclamation into effect.

"Done at Santa Fe the 14th day of September, 1862.   HENRY CONNELLY.

"By the governor:
"W. F. M. Arney,
"Secretary of New Mexico."

The above proclamation recites only the white man's grievances. It says nothing about the injuries received by the Indians at the hands of the whites. It does not refer to the fact that the Mexicans and Americans were at that moment holding more than fifteen hundred Navajo Indians as slaves. Even Governor Connelly himself owned Navajo slaves at the time he wrote the above proclamation. Nor does it relate that the Indians had suffered from the frequent and murderous incursions of the Mexicans; that their flocks had been stolen, their wives and children hunted down and many of them captured and sold into slavery. No, the Indian can not communicate his grievances in so forceful a way as his white neighbors; he remains stolid and silent; he knows it is useless, his story would not be believed anyway. But he had at least one friend among the whites who dared to express his opinion as to the causes of the trouble. This white man bravely fought them and punished them for their wrongs and just as bravely stood up for them in their rights. Let him tell his own story.

Colonel Kit Carson sworn:

I have heard read the statement of Colonel Bent, and his suggestions and opinions in relation to Indian affairs coincide perfectly with my own. I came to this country in 1826, and since that time I have been pretty well acquainted with the Indian tribes, both in peace and at war. I think, as a general thing, the difficulties arise from aggressions on the part of the whites. From what I have heard, the whites are always cursing the Indians, and are not willing to do them justice. For instance, at times large trains come into this country, and some man without any responsibility is hired to guard the horses, mules and stock of the trains; these cattle by his negligence frequently stray off; always, if anything is lost, the cry is raised

Causes of Indian Wars

that the Indians stole it. It is customary among the Indians, even among themselves, if they lose animals, as Indians go everywhere, if they bring them in they expect to get something for their trouble. Among themselves they always pay; but when brought in to this man, who lost them through his negligence, he refuses to pay, and abuses the Indians, striking or sometimes shooting them, because they do not wish to give up the stock without pay; and thus a war is brought on. * * * *

I think if proper men were appointed and proper steps taken, peace could be had with all the Indians on and below the Arkansas, without war. I believe if Colonel Bent and myself were authorized, we could make a solid, lasting peace with those Indians. I have much more confidence in the influence of Colonel Bent with the Indians than in my own. I think if prompt action were taken the Indians could be got together by the tenth of September. I know that even before the acquisition of New Mexico there had about always existed an hereditary warfare between the Navajos and Mexicans; forays were made into each other's country, and stock, women and children stolen. Since the acquisition, the same state has existed; we would hardly get back from fighting and making peace with them before they would be at war again. I consider the reservation system as the only one to be adopted for them.

If they were sent back to their own reservation tomorrow, it would not be a month before hostilities would commence again. There is a part of the Navajos, the wealthy, who wish to live in peace; the poorer class are in the majority, and they have no chiefs who can control them. When I campaigned against them eight months I found them scattered over a country several hundred miles in extent. There is

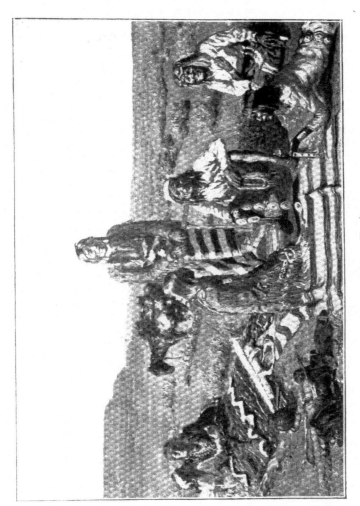

Navajo Indians Trading
(Courtesy of U. S. Hollister)

no suitable place in their own country — and I have
been all over it — where more than two thousand could
here be placed. If located in different places, it would
not be long before they and the Mexicans would be at
war. If they were scattered on different locations, I
hardly think any number of troops could keep them on
their reservations. The mountains they live in in the
Navajo country cannot be penetrated by troops. There
are canyons in their country thirty miles in length,
with walls a thousand feet high, and when at war it
is impossible for troops to pass through these canyons,
in which they hide and cultivate the ground. In the
main Canyon de Chelly they had some two or three
thousand peach trees, which were mostly destroyed by
my troops. Colonel Sumner, in the fall of 1851, went
into the Canyon de Chelly with several hundred men
and two pieces of artillery; he got into the canyon
some eight or ten miles, but had to retreat out of it
at night. In the walls of the canyon they have regular houses built in the crevices, from which they fire
and roll down huge stones on an enemy. They have
regular fortifications, averaging from one to two hundred feet from the bottom, with portholes for firing.
No small arms can injure them, and artillery cannot
be used. In one of these crevices I found a two story
house. I regard these canyons as impregnable. General Canby entered this canyon, but retreated the
next morning. When I captured the Navajos I first
destroyed their crops, and harassed them until the
snow fell very deep in the canyons, taking some prisoners occasionally. I think it was about the 6th of
January, after the snow fell, that I started. Five
thousand soldiers would probably keep them on reservations in their own country. The Navajos had a
good many small herd when I went there. I took
twelve hundred sheep from them at one time, and

smaller lots at different times. The volunteers were allowed one dollar per head for all sheep and goats taken, which were turned over to the commissary. I think General Carleton gave the order as an encouragement to the troops. I think from fifteen hundred to two thousand could subsist themselves in the Valley de Chelly. At this point it took me and three hundred men most one day to destroy a field of corn. I think probably fifteen hundred could subsist on the northeastern slope of the Tunacha mountain. I know of no other place near by where any considerable number could subsist themselves. I was in the valley of the San Juan but can give no idea of the number that could subsist themselves in it. While I was in the country there was continual thieving carried on between the Navajos and Mexicans. Some Mexicans now object to the settlement of the Navajos at the Bosque (Fort Sumner), because they cannot prey on them as formerly. I am of the opinion that, in consequence of the military campaign and the destruction of their crops, they were forced to come in. It appears to me that the only objection to the Bosque is on account of the wood; this consists of mesquite roots.

During the next two years following Governor Connelly's proclamation, over six thousand Navajos were captured by Colonel Kit Carson, **Their Capture** almost without the shedding of blood. He invaded their stronghold, the Canyon de Chelly, a feat that no one before him had ever been able successfully to accomplish. He captured the entire body of Navajos who had retired thither thinking themselves out of all danger. In most instances he was able to reason with them and convince them that their only safety from destruction lay in their peaceably surrendering. His skill in warfare and his indomitable courage and daring won for him the admiration of all the tribes with whom he ever came in contact or to whom his valor and the story of his brave deeds had been carried. The Navajos, however, still delight in telling of the time when they surrounded Kit on top of a large black rock near Fort Defiance and held him there a prisoner for three days, when he finally effected his escape. The name of Kit Carson is to this day held in reverence by all the old members of the Navajo tribe. They say he knew how to be just and considerate as well as how to fight the Indians.

The Navajos were collected and given small tracts of land to cultivate near Fort Sumner, in eastern New Mexico. This section of country **The Bosque Redondo** was called the Bosque Redondo. It proved to be a very unhealthful place for the Navajos, many of them dying from the effects of the alkali water. Wood was also scarce. It consisted largely of the roots of the mesquite bush and had to be dug out of the ground and dried before it would burn readily. This was very hard work and they longed to be permitted to return to their old home where there was plenty of good fuel and where they might tend their flocks, farm their fields and weave their blankets in peace and unmolested quietude.

Serious objections were raised by the citizens of

New Mexico to the government permitting the Navajos to leave the Bosque. It became the topic of the hour throughout the Territory and bitter controversies arose as to the expediency of settling the Navajos again on their old reservation. A Senate committee was finally sent to investigate and report on the condition of these Indians. A council was held with the head-men of the tribe to ascertain their wishes and to know if they had any assurances to offer as to their future conduct if allowed to return. The Indians pleaded pitifully to be allowed to return to the graves of their ancestors and to all they held dear. They told the representatives of the government that all they wished was to be permitted to return unmolested; that they did not ask the government to give them anything, they would manage to live some way. They said if they could be allowed to take one old buck goat back with them this was all they would ask; this goat they would tie to a pinyon tree with leathern thongs on the top of a high mountain when they returned and they would there let him become famished from hunger and thirst, and when the goat should become irritable and angry they would call all the young men of the tribe and place them in a circle about the pinyon tree to which he would be tied, and while the old men incited the animal to madness the young men would look on, and as they watched the goat butt his head against the tree until the blood should ooze from its ears and nose and its head became one mat of gore, they would tell them "thus it is ever, to the Indians who oppose the government.

Navajo Weavers

Fighting the government is all the same as that goat butting the tree. Our sons, take warning, the government is very strong and powerful; the Navajos will ever, hereafter, remain at peace with the government and shall henceforth listen to Washington, for he is our best friend."

So the Navajos, in 1867, were allowed to return to their old reservation. Whether or no the goat incident was ever carried into **Their Return** effect, history does not tell us. **to the Reservation** At any rate the Navajos have ever since kept their word and, except for a few sheep and farming implements, have never received anything from the government. In fact they have refused to have rations issued to them for the reason, they say, they do not want the young men pauperized.

This was the last of the Navajo wars.*

The only treaties ever made with the Navajos were treaties of peace. They have never received an annuity from the government in payment **Treaties** for land ceded because they never owned any land that the white man wanted. This reservation is only a barren waste for the most part, five acres of land being required to support a single sheep. So far, the white man has not coveted the land to any great extent and for this reason, and

*See Appendix.

this reason alone, the Navajos are permitted to roam unmolested over their large reservation and to follow the avocations of peaceful shepherds and farmers in security and undisturbed quietude.

In this the Navajos are extremely fortunate. They are better off in many ways than if they possessed well watered and fertile acres instead of their vast area of desert waste. For nowhere in the United States do we find tribes of Indians who have received large per capita payments for lands sold to the government who have not become greatly demoralized thereby. Outlaws, gamblers and whiskey peddlers have ever followed in the wake of treaty commissions and brought to the simple minded natives diseases, vices and the basest of demoralizing influences, which, in their weakness, they have readily accepted as the refinements of our civilization.

So the Navajos, like the ancient Belgae who dwelt beyond the Marne and Seine, are the bravest, most industrious and independent of any of the tribes of North American Indians, for the reason that they do not receive the annual gift of gold from the government to attract to their reservation the lawless and depraved characters who would import those vices and customs which tend to enervate both mind and body.

CHAPTER VI
Their Religion and Morals

The Navajo is intensely and even intemperately religious. He is a great pantheist and ascribes the attributes of Divinity to all the mighty **A Pantheist** manifestations of nature. He believes in a Great Spirit — the All of All — but contemplates Him only as some mysterious, mighty power whose anger must be appeased by prayer and supplication. The following is one of his prayers, according to Dr. Matthews:

Reared within the Mountains!
Lord of the Mountains!
Young Man!
Chieftain!
I have made your sacrifices,
I have prepared a smoke for you.
My feet restore thou me.
My legs restore thou me.
My body restore thou me.
My mind restore thou me.
My voice restore thou me.
Restore all for me in beauty.
Make beautiful all that is before me.
Make beautiful all that is behind me.
Make beautiful my words.
It is done in beauty.
It is done in beauty.
It is done in beauty.
It is done in beauty.

This is a prayer addressed to the prophet Dsilyi Neyani in the great ceremony of the Mountain Chant, an elaborate religious rite of nine days duration which the Navajos celebrate ostensibly for the healing of the sick. The supplicant after offering the sacrificial sticks smoked the sacrificial cigarette and this was the smoke he had prepared for the prophet.*

The Navajo's heaven is below, not in the skies above. It is said that he believes that all departed spirits go to a marsh or swamp, where they remain for four days. If they have always obeyed the gods they will be shown a ladder leading them to a world below. Some of their people never reach this place, but are lost forever. They worship two great spirits, male and female, or father and mother. These dwell at the rising and setting of the sun. After descending the ladder they enter the new world. Here they behold their father and mother combing their hair. This they look upon in silence for several days, when they climb the ladder back up into the swamp to bathe and become purified. Then they return to the world below and to where they first saw the two spirits combing their hair. In this world they remain for eternity, contented and happy.

Like all Indians, the Navajos are a very superstitious people. They use charms for almost everything. Of these they have great num-
Superstition bers. For rain they use a long round stone which they believe falls from the clouds when it thunders. They use bear's gall which they dry in the sun and carry about their person in

*For full description of the ceremony of the Mountain Chant see *5th Annual Report Bureau of American Ethnology.*

A Navajo Winter Hogan

(From the *Southern Workman*)

small buck-skin bags to keep away the witches. For the cure of common diseases they use feathers, stones, crane's bills, antelope toes, roots, leaves, etc.

The Navajo's religion is to be found in his great rites and ceremonies, commonly called dances. Many of these are elaborate and require several days in their performance. In performing his rites there is much praying and offering of sacrifices. These sacrifices are always of an innocent nature — no shedding of blood. None of his great religious ceremonies has ever been thoroughly understood by the white man and doubtless never will be, but we do know that the Navajo is a very religious being though his faith could hardly be classed as orthodox.

The Navajo reservation has an area almost equal to one-third the state of Pennsylvania, with an estimated population of 20,000 to 28,000 In-
Morals dians, and if they were so inclined they could commit all manner of crimes among themselves without fear of punishment. But they do not do so. They gamble a great deal but they seldom have any disputes among themselves over their games. The women are generally virtuous and are perhaps the most independent wives to be found among any of the Indian tribes on the continent. Owning the children and the sheep in their own right, they are in a position to demand a hearing in deciding all the important matters pertaining to the domestic welfare of the family.

Nor does the Navajo as a rule indulge in the use of

intoxicating beverages. His only stimulating beverage is coffee—Arbuckle's roasted coffee—"the drink that cheers but does not inebriate." He will use no other brand. There appears to be something about this particular brand of coffee that is very pleasing to the Navajo palate and he stubbornly refuses to accept a substitute. Wherever Indians can be found who have not given themselves up to the white man's fire water, they are almost always harmless and peaceable people. Few tribes can now be found in the United States in which great numbers of the men, and even many of the women, do not drink intoxicating liquors to excess. There is no such thing as moderation when it comes to drinking whiskey with an Indian. He drinks it to get drunk and he gets drunk. The Navajos are perhaps as free from the curse as any tribe now to be found in our country, and as a result we find them generally free from evil vices and immoral practices. There is not a community of people of equal number in the world more law abiding, peaceable and industrious as a class than the Navajo Indians.

CHAPTER VII

Navajo Mythology

Navajo mythology is replete with legends handed down from father to son telling the origin of every good and evil thing known to **Myth and Tradition** his simple life. While he does not contemplate a First Great Cause or its attendant effect, yet his legends contain the story of the creation of his present world, — the sun, moon, stars, sky, rivers, mountains, cliffs and canyons. He has a legend of a flood which destroyed all the wicked people. There is also the Wind god, Rain god, War god, etc., to whom he attributes omnipotent powers.

While the Navajo has produced no literature and has no great epics or lyrics, still he has created elaborate dramas. All of his dramas are founded on myths. Many of these myths are very long so that perhaps few Navajos know thoroughly more than two or three of the great myths. Like the myths of most all other people, they may be either explanatory, such as attempt to explain the mysteries of existence and universal life; aesthetic, those designed to elicit emotion and give pleasure; or the romantic myth, which displays the character of some favorite hero. In Navajo mythology may be found all of these classes of myths. We will not here con-

sider the stage of the Navajo myth, whether in the
hecastotheism, zootheism, physitheism or psychotheism
stage.

A few of his myths, taken from acknowledged
authorities, follow:

CREATION OF THE FIRST MAN AND WOMAN
(According to Dr. Matthews)
The gods laid a buckskin on the ground with the
head to the west; on this they placed two ears of
corn, one yellow, one white,
Some Navajo Myths with their tips to the east;
and over the corn they spread
another buckskin with its head to the east; under
the white ear they put the feather of a white
eagle, under the yellow ear the feather of a yellow eagle. Then the white wind blew from the
east and the yellow wind blew from the west, between the skins. While the wind was blowing, eight
of the Mirage People came and walked around the objects on the ground four times, and as they walked the
eagle feathers, whose tips protruded from between the
buckskins, were seen to move. When the Mirage
People had finished their walk the upper buckskin
was lifted, — the ears of corn had disappeared; a man
and a woman lay there in their stead. The white ear
of corn had been changed into a man, the yellow ear
into a woman.

The pair thus created were First Man and First
Woman.

MYTH OF THE OLD MAN AND WOMAN OF THE FIRST WORLD
(According to Stevenson)
In the lower world four gods were created by
Etseastin and Etseasun. These gods were so annoyed by
the ants that they said, ''Let us go to the four points

of the world.'' A spring was found at each of the cardinal points, and each god took possession of a spring, which he jealously guarded.

Etseastin and Etseasun were jealous because they had no water and they needed some to produce nourishment. The old man finally obtained a little water from each of the gods and planted it, and from it he raised a spring such as the gods had. From this spring came corn and other vegetation. Etseastin and Etseasun sat on opposite sides of the spring facing each other, and sang and prayed and talked to somebody about themselves, and thus they originated worship. One day the old man saw some kind of fruit in the middle of the spring. He tried to reach it but he could not, and asked the spider woman (a member of his family) to get it for him. She spun a web across the water and by its use procured the fruit, which proved to be a large white shell, quite as large as a Tusayan basket. The following day Etseastin discovered another kind of fruit in the spring which the spider woman also brought him; this fruit was the turquoise. The third day still another kind of fruit was discovered by him and obtained by the spider woman; this was the abalone shell. The fourth day produced the black stone bead, which was also procured.

After ascending into the upper world Etseastin visited the four corners to see what he could find. (They had brought a bit of everything from the lower world with them.) From the east he brought eagle feathers; from the south feathers from the blue-jay; in the west he found hawk feathers, and in the north speckled nightbird (whippoorwill) feathers. Etseastin and Etseasun carried these to a spring, placing them toward the cardinal points. The eagle plumes were laid to the east and near by them white corn and white shell; the blue feathers were laid to the south with blue corn and turquoise; the hawk feathers were laid to the west with yellow corn and abalone shell; and to the north were laid the whippoorwill feathers with black beads and corn of all the several colors. The old man and woman sang and prayed as they had done at the spring in the lower world. They prayed to the east and the white wolf was created; to the south, and the otter appeared; to the west, and the mountain lion came; and to the north, the beaver. Etseastin made these animals rulers over the several points from which they came.

When the white of daylight met the yellow of sunset in mid-heavens they embraced, and white gave birth to the coyote; yellow to the yellow fox. Blue of the south and black of the north similarly met, giving birth, blue to blue fox and north to badger.

Blue and yellow foxes were given to the Pueblos; coyote and badgers remain with the Navajo; but Great Wolf is ruler over them all. Great Wolf was the chief who counseled separation of the sexes.

THE CREATION OF THE SUN

(According to Stevenson)

The first three worlds were neither good nor healthful. They moved all the time and made the people dizzy. Upon ascending into this world the Navajos found only darkness and they said, "We must have light."

In the Ure Mountains lived two women, Ahsonnutli, the turquoise hermaphrodite, and Yolaikaiason, the white shell woman. These two women were sent for by the Navajo, who told them they wished light. The Navajo had already partially separated light into its several colors. Next to the floor was white indicating dawn, upon the white blue was spread for morning, and on the blue yellow for sunset, and next was black representing night. They had prayed long and continuously over these, but their prayers had availed nothing. The two women on arriving told the people to have patience and their prayers would eventually be answered.

Night had a familiar, who was always at his ear. This person said, "Send for the youth at the great falls." Night sent as his messenger a shooting star. The youth soon appeared and said, "Ahsonnutli, the hermaphrodite, has white beads in her right breast and turquoise in her left. We will tell her to lay them on darkness and see what she can do with her prayers." This she did. The youth from the great falls said to Ahsonnutli, "You have carried the white shell beads and turquoise a long time; you should know what to say." Then with a crystal dipped in pollen she marked eyes and mouth on the turquoise and on the white shell-beads, and forming a circle around these with the crystal she produced a slight light from the white-shell bead and a greater light from the turquoise, but the light was insufficient.

Twelve men lived at each of the cardinal points. The forty-eight men were sent for. After their arrival Ahsonnutli sang a song, the men sitting opposite to her; yet even with their presence the song failed to secure the needed light. Two eagle plumes were placed upon each cheek of the turquoise and two on the cheeks of the white-shell beads and one at each of the cardinal points. The twelve men of the east placed twelve turquoises at the east of the faces. The twelve men of the south placed twelve white-shell beads at the south. The twelve men of the west placed twelve turquoises at the west. Those of the north placed twelve white shelled beads at that point. Then with the crystal dipped in corn pollen they made a circle embracing the whole. The wish still remained unrealized. Then Ahsonnutli held the crystal over the turquoise face, whereupon it lighted into a blaze. The people retreated far back on account of the great heat, which continued increasing. The men from the four points found the heat so intense that they arose, but they could hardly stand, as the heavens were so close to them. They looked up and saw two rainbows, one across the other from east to west, and from north to south. The heads and feet of the rainbows almost touched the men's heads. The men tried to raise the great light, but each time they failed. Finally a man and woman appeared, whence they knew not. The man's name was Atseatsine and the woman's name was Atseatsan. They were asked, "How can this sun be got up." They replied, "We know; we heard the people down here trying to raise it, and this is why we came." "Chanteen" (sun's rays), exclaimed the man, "I have the chanteen; I have a crystal from which I can light the chanteen, and I have the rainbow; with these three I can raise the sun." The people said, "Go ahead and raise it." When he had elevated the sun a short distance it tipped a little and burned vegetation and scorched the people, for it was still too near. Then the people said to Atseatsine and Atseatsan, "Raise the sun higher," and they continued to elevate it, and yet it continued to burn everything. They were then called upon to "lift it higher still, as high as possible," but after a certain height was reached their power failed; it would go no farther.

The couple then made four poles, two of turquoise and two of white-shell beads, and each was put under the sun, and with these poles the twelve men at each of the cardinal points raised it. They could not get it high enough to prevent the people and grass from burning. The people then said, "Let us stretch the world"; so the twelve men at each point expanded the world. The sun continued to rise as the world expanded, and began to shine with less heat, but when

A Navajo Head Man

it reached the meridian the heat became great and the
people suffered much. They crawled everywhere to
find shade. Then the voice of Darkness went four
times around the world telling the men at the cardinal points to go on expanding the world. "I want
all this trouble stopped," said Darkness; "the people
are suffering and all is burning; you must continue
stretching." And the men blew and stretched, and
after a time they saw the sun rise beautifully, and
when the sun again reached the meridian it was only
tropical. It was then just right, and as far as the
eye could reach the earth was encircled first with the
white dawn of day, then with the blue of early morning, and all things were perfect. And Ahsonnutli
commanded the twelve men to go to the east, south,
west and north, to hold up the heavens, which office
they are supposed to perform to this day.

CHAPTER VIII

Ceremonies

The Navajos have a great many ceremonies which they practice with as much earnestness and devotion as was the custom of their fathers **Ha-tal-i** before them. Many of their ceremonies, which are usually performed for the healing of the sick, are very long, elaborate and intricate rites, being often of nine days duration. The priest of the ceremony is called *ha-tal-i,* which signifies chanter, or singer. It requires many years of patient work to learn one of the great rites perfectly, there being in many of them more than two hundred different songs to be memorized, and no priest attempts to learn more than one of the great rites, though he may know some of the rites of many of the minor ceremonies.

In many of their ceremonies the Navajos masquerade in the paraphernalia of their favorite gods, and while posing as a god they may gesticulate and utter strange sounds yet they must never speak. The Navajo is for the time being, to all intents and purposes, the god he represents himself to be, and he hears prayers and accepts sacrifices, not as a Navajo, but as the god he is impersonating. He deceives no one, but acts simply as an impersonator of divinity, much the same as the priests of our Christian churches do when

they receive offerings, hear confessions and dispense
blessings.

The ceremony of the Mountain Chant is perhaps
one of the most elaborate rites celebrated by the Navajos. It is founded on a myth,
The Mountain Chant   the burden of which is the
story of the wanderings of
a family of six Navajos, the father, mother, two sons
and two daughters. These people wandered for many
days in the vicinity of the Carrizo mountains, then
journeyed far to the north, crossing the San Juan
river. The legend relates that the two sons provided
meat for the family by hunting rabbits, wood rats
and other small animals, and how the two daughters
gathered edible seeds and roots on the way. It was
a long time before the young men learned to follow
the trail of the deer, and on one occasion, after returning to camp without the coveted deer, the old man
became much provoked at the stupidity of his sons and
said to them, "You kill nothing because you know
nothing. If you had knowledge you would be successful. I pity you." He then directed them to build a
sweat-house, giving them instructions as to the details
of its construction. After undergoing the purifying
ordeal of the sweat bath, he began slowly and carefully
to teach them all the arts of wood-craft; how to sur-
prise the vigilant deer, and carefully, step by step,
they were initiated into the mysteries of the chase. After many days of careful drilling, these sons made
great preparations for going on a big hunt in the dis-

tant mountains. They returned after many days, each
with a deer he had slain, together with much dried
meat and many skins.

It finally developed that the old man was a great
prophet, and the myth goes on to relate how the two
sons disobeyed their father's instructions and the punishment that was visited upon them by the gods in
consequence thereof. Afterwards the prophet was
captured by the Utes, always at enmity with the
Navajos, bound hand and foot and sentenced by the
Ute council to be whipped to death. An angel visited
the old man in the night and unloosed his thongs and
the prophet took his flight, and after undergoing many
hair-breadth escapes finally reached the home of the
gods who taught him how to make offerings to the
deities. They also taught him the mysteries of the
dry sand-paintings, and how to perform the great
healing rites of the Mountain Chant.

When the prophet at last returned to his people,
a great feast and dance was given in his honor. There
was much rejoicing and making merry. He was washed
from head to foot and dried with the sacred corn meal.
He was then asked to relate his experiences in the
strange land of the gods. He now proceeded to teach
his people the new rites he had learned from the gods
and the preparation and use of the sacrificial sticks.
A day was appointed when this new ceremony would
be performed; all the neighboring tribes were invited
to attend and there was much rejoicing and exchang-
ing of friendly good will. The ceremony was contin-

ued through nine days and nights, at the conclusion of which the prophet vanished in the air and was seen no more on earth.

And this is the account the Navajos give of the origin of the ceremony of the Mountain Chant.

This ceremony is, in reality, a great passion play. The costumes are numerous and elaborate. There is much dancing, so called, but it is really not dancing at all, simply the acting out of the drama of the great cosmic myth in prepetuating the religious symbols of the tribe.

The following description of the ''Fire Play'' is taken from Dr. Washington Matthews:

The eleventh dance was the fire dance, or fire play, which was the most picturesque and startling of all. Every man except the leader **The Fire Play** bore a long, thick bundle of shredded cedar bark in each hand and one had two extra bundles on his shoulders for the later use of the leader. The latter carried four small fagots of the same material in his hands. Four times they all danced around the fire, waving their bundles of bark toward it. They halted in the east; the leader advanced towards the central fire, lighted one of his fagots, and trumpeting loudly threw it to the east over the fence of the corral. He performed a similar act at the south, at the west, and at the north; but before the northern brand was thrown he lighted with it the bark bundles of his comrades. As each brand disappeared over the fence some of the spectators blew into their hands and made a motion as if tossing some substance into the departing flame. When the fascicles were all lighted the whole band began a wild race around the fire. At first they kept close together and spat upon one another some substance of supposed medicinal virtue. Soon they scattered and ran apparently without concert, the rapid racing causing the brands to throw out long brilliant streamers of flame over the hands and arms of the dancers. Then they proceeded to apply the brands to their own nude bodies and to the bodies of their comrades in front of them, no man ever once turning around; at times the dancer struck his victim vigorous blows with his flaming wand; again he seized the flame as if it were a sponge, and, keeping close to the one pursued, rubbed the back of the latter for several moments, as if he were bathing him. In the meantime the sufferer would perhaps catch up with some one in front of him and in turn bathe him in flame. At times when a dancer found no one in front of him he proceeded to sponge his own back, and might keep this up while making two or three circuits around the fire or until he caught up with some one else. At each application of the blaze the loud trumpeting was heard, and it often seemed as if a great flock of cranes was winging its way over head southward through the darkness. If a brand became extinguished it was lighted again in the central fire; but when it was so far consumed as to be no longer held conveniently in the hand, the dancer dropped it and rushed, trumpeting, out of the corral. Thus, one by one, they all departed. When they were gone many of the spectators came forward, picked up some of the fallen fragments of cedar bark, lighted them, and bathed their hands in the flames as a charm against the evil effects of fire.

The Hoshkawn Dance, the Plumed Arrow Dance and the Wand Dance are some of the other important ceremonies in the great rite of the Mountain Chant. Few white people, except those living in the immediate vicinity of the Navajos, have ever witnessed many of the Navajo ceremonies for the reason that as these ceremonies are primarily for the healing of the sick, no regular time for holding them is ever appointed by the priests. When a Navajo gets sick it is necessary for his friends and relatives to hold a consultation and decide on what one of the many ceremonies will most likely effect a cure. This decided, a theurgist is selected who is familiar with the rites to be performed and he is immediately sought out and bargained with. The patient pays all the expenses of the ceremony which is often a very elaborate affair and very expensive. All visitors are expected to feast, make merry and have a good time, at the expense of the patient.

One of the most interesting features, to the casual observer of the great religious ceremonies of the Navajos, is the elaborate paintings with **Sand Paintings** various colored dry sands. Careful preparations are made in the lodge by covering the floor with a coating of sand about three inches in thickness. A black pigment is then prepared from charcoal for the black, yellow sandstone for the yellow, red sandstone for the red and white sandstone for the white. A kind of blue is made by mixing the black with the yellow.

Before beginning the painting the surface of the sand is carefully smoothed with a broad oaken batten.

Young men usually do the painting under the careful and ever watchful eye of the shaman.   There is a set rule which must be followed in each of the four great paintings.   The Navajo shaman believes that to depart from the fixed order as handed down from father to son through many generations, would be to invite the enmity of the gods.   The true design must be followed, although within certain limits the artist may display his skill.

In order to understand these sand paintings it is necessary to know thoroughly the myths upon which they are based.   Perhaps no white man has ever yet been able fully to understand and appreciate their symbolism.   Since the Navajos do not preserve any patterns to go by, it is wonderful how they are enabled to preserve all the details of these elaborate paintings. Yet they claim not to have varied in any essential detail in all these hundreds of years.

A Navajo Silversmith

CHAPTER IX

Their Arts and Crafts

History of the Art of Weaving From a marauding robber and relentless warrior, to a peace-loving industrious producer, is the evolution of the Navajo Indian. A little more than forty years ago he was an outlaw, requiring a regiment of armed men to keep him in subjection. The Navajo had energy plus. He was always doing something, mostly something bad. His character was the product of his own misdirected energy. It required, as we have seen, the strategy of Kit Carson and hundreds of trained soldiers to teach him the lesson of respectful obedience to lawful authority, and to convince him that his rights ceased where the rights of others began.

About the year 1675 the various Pueblo tribes formed a coalition for the overthrow of Spanish dominion in New Mexico and Arizona, and the day of retribution came in 1680, for it was in that year that they drove the Spaniards from their land, killing and destroying everything that reminded them of Spanish oppression. When the Spaniards returned a few years later carrying their bloody inquisitions into these defenseless Pueblo villages, many of the inhabitants were unable successfully to resist the iniquities that were perpetrated against them and so a great many of the Pueblos fled to the Navajos for protection.

At this time the Navajos depended chiefly upon the spoils of conquest for their support. They toiled not, neither did they spin. Their neighbors, the Pueblos, did both. They raised corn and cotton in the valleys, and when the crops were gathered they carried them up the steep mesas and stored their food and fiber away in the hidden recesses of their pueblos for safe keeping, to be used as occasion required. Their corn furnished them food for winter and their cotton they wove into blankets, ceremonial belts and into cloth for clothing. The Navajos found these peaceful, industrious Pueblo Indians an easy prey, and often laid waste their fields and plundered their villages.

With the Navajo it has been the survival of the fittest. The outlaws and daring marauders of other tribes were attracted to them by common interests. Only the strong, brave and mentally alert could keep pace with the bold, reckless Navajos, hence the weak, feeble and decrepit fell by the wayside. Being thus subjected to the weeding out process, as the years went by the tribe grew strong, both mentally and physically.

We have already stated that the Navajo can give no intelligent account of his ancestry or of the country from whence he came. His past history is practically a blank. He, like all other races of mankind, is a simple sequence. He is what he is to-day because he did what he did in days gone by. But for the coming of the Spaniard his history might be very different. He possessed neither horse, sheep, goats nor cattle, but either by barter or stealth he early came into possession of them. The Spaniards brought sheep into his country and thenceforth the Navajos were to be the greatest aboriginal pastoral people in the New World.

As long as the Navajo carried on aggressive warfare he made little progress in the arts of peace. Not until the oppressed of the more peaceful and progressive sedentary tribes began to flee to him for protection, did he take up any of the important handicrafts which now distinguish him so signally from other Indians. The Pueblos raised cotton and wove it into cloth, but the Navajo knew nothing about weaving before the introduction of sheep by the Spaniards. He did not grow cotton, nor is it anywhere evident that he knew the first principles of manufacturing raw material into finished products. He evidently learned the art of weaving from the Pueblos who fled to him for protection from the horrors of the Spanish Inquisition.

While the Navajos give considerable attention to agriculture and the raising of horses and cattle, still the principal industry among them is the growing of sheep. It is a poor family, indeed, that does not possess a flock of sheep and goats. Goats are to be found in almost every Navajo herd. They are prized by them chiefly for their flesh and pelts. Goats are also desirable additions to their flocks from their habit of leading out and scattering the sheep sufficiently to graze over a large area which is necessary for the best development of flocks in the Navajo country where five acres of land is required to support a single sheep. The Navajos also claim that goats are useful in protecting the sheep from attacks by wolves and coyotes. The goat will show fight while the sheep meekly submits to his fate.

While the Navajo has always possessed marked tribal characteristics that have attracted the attention of tourists and ethnologists for a great many years, it is his native wool blanket that has given him an universal reputation. Every honest person and every lover of true art, admires truth expressed in the creation of the mind and in the product of the hand. Beauty and utility are the marked characteristics of the Navajo blanket. Our North American Indians have, as a rule, produced very little that the average white man considers useful to present-day civilization. Some tribes, like the Sioux and Ojibways, do beautiful bead work, the Pueblos make artistic pottery, and several tribes in Arizona and California make beautiful baskets. But the white man has little use for these things and if he purchases them at all, which he often does, it is simply to please his fancy and to satisfy his craving for something Indian. We have witnessed, during the past few years, the "Indian fad," taking the country almost by storm. There has been a great demand for all sorts of Indian handiwork. All sorts of Indian purses and moccasins, manufactured in large quantities in the East, have been placed on the market by enterprising dealers. The various Indian tribes throughout the west also make a great many things simply to sell to tourists. The Indian finds in this work an occupation that is congenial to him as well as a source of income, and the tourist gets what he wants, "a genuine Indian curio" to take back home with him as material evidence that he has seen a "sure-enough" Indian.

But it is quite different with the Navajo blanket. This possesses intrinsic value. While many people believe these blankets are made in Eastern factories by the "Yankees" and shipped to Western traders to deceive "tenderfoot" tourists, this is a mistake. The Indian buys the factory made blanket for his own use. The Mackinaw robes are worn by all "blanket" Indians. They are usually of bright colors and elaborate pattern, the designs being often taken from Navajo blankets and other Indian handicraft.

It may not be generally known, but it is a fact, nevertheless, that the Navajo does not wear his own make of blankets. They are too valuable, for one reason, since one Navajo blanket of good weave and pattern, is worth half a dozen ordinary Indian robes sold by the trader. Another reason is that the Navajo blanket is too heavy and cumbersome to wear as a robe. The Indian much prefers the factory made blanket for his own use, and if we wore blankets as he does, I am sure we would prefer them also. We should soon grow very weary of carrying a ten or fifteen pound Navajo blanket around our shoulders; besides they are very stiff and do not easily adjust themselves to the form of the body, a quality very desirable in a robe of any sort.

The art of weaving is comparatively a new art among the Navajos. As previously stated they learned it from the Pueblos and since the introduction of sheep into their country by the Spaniards. It is certainly not more than three hundred years since they began to weave, if it is that long. The Pueblos were fine weavers of cloth and they still do very fine weaving, but it is in the weaving of blankets or rugs, that the Navajo excels. We naturally admire the happy faculty of "catching on" in any people. The fact that the Navajo, who had always been a warrior and little given to useful toil, should take up the craft of a people that he naturally despised and held in contempt, and so excel him in the application of that art as to practically take it out of his hands, is worthy of the emulation of the highest civilized people in the world.

A genuine Navajo blanket is hand made from start to finish. The Indian grows his own wool, cards it, spins it, dyes it, and weaves it, all by hand in the most primitive manner. He formerly pulled the wool from the sheep with his hands but with the advent of the trader came the common sheep-shears, and he at once began the use of them. Were you to visit a Navajo weaver's hogan or lodge, you would expect to see a large old fashioned loom and spinning wheel something like those our great grandmothers used in making what they called "home-spun cloth," but you would, in reality, see very different appliances employed in carrying on this textile industry. By comparison the loom and spinning wheel of our Colonial ancestors were as intricate and complicated as the machinery of a modern woolen mill. The Navajo spinning wheel consists of a small wooden spindle made of hard wood, and about eighteen inches in length, on which is fastened a wooden disc three or four inches in diameter. This spindle is dextrously twirled with the fingers, while the soft wool, which has been carded with a pair of old fashioned hand cards into small rolls, is twisted into smooth, strong threads. Often this process is repeated four or five times in order to secure the desired smoothness, tenacity and fineness in the yarn. Think of the labor required in the very first processes. After the spinning the yarn must be dyed. Formerly native vegetable dyes were used exclusively. These vegetable dyes never faded but grew more mellow and beautiful with age. It is to be deplored that the ordinary dyes of commerce have largely taken the place of the vegetable dyes in the manufacture of the Navajo blanket. The best weavers still use some of the common colors in the vegetable dyes in connection with the analine dyes to make the latter "set." Perhaps the main reason for discarding the vegetable dyes by the Navajo weavers is the fact that they find it much cheaper and by far less work to use the commercial dyes. They also get a greater variety of colors. In their native dyes they never had very many different colors. They had a beautiful yellow which they made from a yellow flower that grows in their country. But they had no red such as they now get with the dyes of commerce, except as they purchased the bayeta cloth from the Spanish traders.

This was their first bright red. It cost them six dollars per pound and was used sparingly. These old bayeta blankets are now very scarce and command high prices.

The inventive genius of the white man has never yet been able to reproduce the Navajo effect in a blanket. In the white man's loom when a color starts across the beam it must be carried all the way across and appear on one side or the other in the finished product. Not so with the Navajo loom. This loom is, if possible, even more primitive than the old fashioned spinning spindle. Ordinarily two forked posts driven into the ground with a cross beam supported in the crotches, serves for the frame. The chain or warp is then fastened in this frame and sitting flat on the ground, the weaver picks up a ball of yarn and using her hand as a shuttle she starts across the beam, cutting out one color and substituting another anywhere she desires. This gives her unlimited range for color and design. The Mexican Indians have a very rudely constructed loom, something like the old time rag carpet loom on which they weave a blanket that looks something like the Navajo product. But in reality it is very different. In the first place, these Mexican rugs are of uniform size, as they have to have a different loom for each size of rug made. They are also of a very loose, slazy weave as compared to the tight, firm weave of the better grade of Navajo blankets. Several blankets are woven on the same chain, which is cotton, and are cut apart something like towels, leaving a fringe at the ends which is tied or

Navajo Women Shearing Sheep

braided to prevent raveling. They are often sold for
genuine Navajo blankets, but they are in every way
inferior to them.

There are as many patterns and designs as there
are blankets themselves, no two ever being exactly
alike. One very striking peculiarity about every Navajo blanket is its incompleteness. There is a superstition prevailing among the Navajos, more inexorable
than law, that perfection means the end. They believe that if they should weave a perfectly symmetrical
blanket, with all the designs carried out to perfect
completeness, this would be the last blanket they
would ever live to weave. Hence an extra stripe, a
larger figure or some peculiar blending of colors or
curiously wrought design will invariably appear somewhere in every blanket, though to the untutored eye
it is difficult to detect it in the finer weaves.

Perhaps the most striking pattern woven by the
Navajos is what is familiarly known as the "Old Chief
Design," or Hon-el-chod-di. This differs from all
other designs in many ways. First, it is wider than
long, the woof being about one and one half times as
long as the warp. The colors in this pattern are
white, black, navy blue and red in the order named.
In some instances the navy blue is omitted and in
others the black. The pattern is alternating black
and white bars, four or six inches wide, extending
across the blanket, with one long diamond in the
center, and four half-diamonds mid-way of the top
and bottom and on each side, and a quarter diamond
woven on each of the four corners. A dark field of

black, red and blue generally connects the central diamond with each of the half-diamonds to the right and left. In olden times, when the Navajos wore their own make of blankets, only the chiefs of the tribe were permitted to wear a *hon-el-chod-di* blanket.

It might be well to state here that all weaving among the Navajos is done by the women, but among the Pueblo Indians the men are the weavers. There is on the Navajo reservation a hermaphrodite who weaves blankets. He weaves only one blanket each year and this is always a very large, fine one. It is a marked characteristic of the hermaphrodites among the Navajos that they are always more dextrous at woman's work than are the women themselves. According to Navajo mythology the First Man and the First Woman were created from two ears of corn and the first fruits of their marriage were twins and hermaphrodites. There is a prevailing superstition among the Navajos, therefore, that the hermaphrodite is possessed of supernatural powers, and the hermaphrodite here referred to is a noted shaman, or medicine man, of the tribe.

The Navajo weaver does not have a pattern to go by, but makes up her design as she goes along. These designs reflect, largely, the state of her mind at the time and the power of her imagination. During late years, since the wishes of the whites have created a demand for striking designs, many sacred emblems of the great religious ceremonies are woven into the blankets. Oftentimes they are very intricate and if they could be read would unfold many a sacred rite or

legend and reveal the thoughts of the imaginative
soul who so silently and patiently weaves her life and
character into her blanket.

The following tribute to the Navajo weaver is
from the pen of Edwin L. Sabin:

Out in the land of little rain;
Of cactus-rift and canyon plain,
An Indian woman, short and swart,
This blanket wove with patient art;
And day to day, through all a year,
Before her loom, by patterns queer,
She stolidly a story told,
A legend of her people, old.

With thread on thread and line on line,
She wrought each curious design,
The symbol of the day and night.
Of desert dark and of mountain height,
Of journey long and storm beset,
Of village passed and dangers met,
Of wind and season, cold and heat,
Of famine harsh and plenty sweet.

Now in this pale-face home it lies,
'Neath careless, unsuspecting eyes,
Which never read the tale that runs
A course of ancient, mystic suns,
To us 'tis simply many-hued,
Of figures barbarous and rude;
Appeals in vain its pictured lore;
An Indian blanket — nothing more.

While the Navajo women are the weavers of the tribe, her liege lord displays his skill and art as a craftsman in fashioning from silver **The Pesh-li-kai,** coins the many ornaments used for **or Silversmith** personal adornment of both sexes.

He is an improvident Navajo, indeed, who does not possess one or more articles of the *pesh-li-kai's* manufacture.

Silver rings, bracelets, ear-rings, necklaces, stick pins, belts, buttons, buckles and various other ornaments for his person and paraphernalia all curiously hand chased and tooled, and often set with native stone settings of turquoise and garnets, or with imported opals, turquoise, sapphires, amethysts, etc., are the chief products of his handicraft. He also makes silver bridle heads for ornamenting his pony, which are often worth two or three times as much as the horse upon which they are to be worn. Souvenir silver spoons of various designs are made by him which he sells to the Indian traders.

His tools are often of the rudest sort and considering the advantages he has for studying designs from observation, much less of seeing skilled silversmiths at work in their modern, well equipped shops, the skill and originality displayed in the manufacture of his jewelry is really very remarkable. But we must remember the Navajo has initiative. He will undertake to do almost anything he has ever seen a white man do. He probably learned the art of working in metals from the early Spanish explorers, but

Navajo Jewelry
(Courtesy of J. B. Moore)

Navajo Silverware
(Courtesy of J. B. Moore)

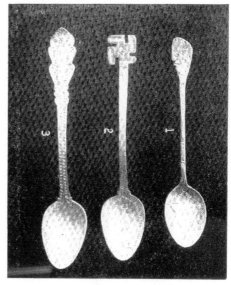

Navajo Silverware
(Courtesy of J. B. Moore)

it is safe to assume that he has had very little instruction along these lines, for he has not yet learned the use of the baser metals. He uses only silver coins in the manufacture of his jewelry and silver-ware. Nothing but the genuine satisfies the Navajo.

REMOVE

THIS

WRITING

CHAPTER X

Civilization

From the view point of the casual observer the Navajo Indian is simply an ignorant, superstitious but industrious barbarian. He will **As viewed by the White Man** have none of the white man's religion, his own being good enough for him. He does not object to missionaries, but he wants them to come to him with a tool chest and a practical knowledge of agriculture by irrigation, and of stock raising. He protests that he knows nothing about "that man up in the skies" and of that world where there will be no more work. On one occasion a committee of Navajos called upon their agent and entered a protest against their missionary. They said they were tired of hearing about a world up in the skies where there would be lots to eat and nothing to do; they said they could not understand about the white man's heaven, nor about that Jesus man whose home was away up in the skies somewhere, but that they could understand about the things in this life and in this world and that they wanted a new missionary — one who could teach them a better way of living their life here on earth, a better way of farming their lands, how to improve the breeds of their flocks and herds, how to repair their plows and harness, and how to mend a broken wagon. These, they said, were the qualifications of the missionary that would be able to help the Navajos, but as to the Bible, they knew nothing about that and could not understand its teachings; it was made for the white people and not for the Navajos.

To the orthodox missionary, his is a hopeless case, or well nigh hopeless — a heathen and a pagan beyond redemption. Not very many years ago and he would have suffered death by burning at the stake for such heresy and even though a savage he would have either been converted or killed. And indeed it is extremely doubtful if the Navajo ever attains to anything approaching our civilization until he does accept those fundamental truths of Christianity as taught on the shores of Galilee by the lowly Nazarene. He needs a little more charity, a little more brotherly love and a little less adherence to the old Scriptural injunction — an eye for an eye and a tooth for a tooth. He is a diamond in the rough.

The Navajo is now sending his children to school, the Government maintaining several industrial training schools on his reservation for their education. He is turning his mechanical aptitude to account by finding employment in machine shops and at the stone mason's trade in neighboring towns. Others secure work on the railroads as section hands and in the sugar beet fields as day laborers. The blanket weavers and the silversmiths are constantly employed and the product of their handicraft finds ready sale

His Progress

at goodly prices, their blankets being in great demand throughout the United States and even in foreign countries. From their sheep, goats, cattle and sale of their blankets the Navajos have a yearly income of from six hundred to ten hundred thousand dollars. The Government is making an effort to develop water for them for irrigation purposes and for their stock, is improving their sheep by cross-breeding and is providing work for them whereby they can add to their income while at the same time they develop and maintain their splendid independence and initiative of which they are justly so proud.

It is safe to assume that the Navajo Indian will always remain an INDIAN. He shows no disposition to amalgamate with any other race. Dur-
His Future ing the past few years the policy of the government has been to study the characteristics of the Indian and to adopt such measures as will most likely tend toward the development of all his natural instincts along lines calculated to make him a better Indian.

In a recent annual report to the Secretary of the Department of the Interior, Mr. Francis E. Leupp, Commissioner of Indian Affairs, said:

The Indian is a natural warrior, a natural logician, a natural artist. We have room for all three in our highly organized social system. Let us not make the mistake, in the process of absorbing them, of washing out of them whatever is distinctly INDIAN. Our aboriginal brother brings, as his contribution to the

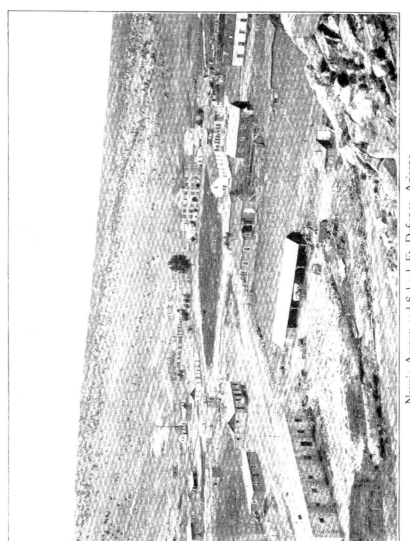

Navajo Agency and School, Ft. Defiance, Arizona

common store of character, a great deal which is admirable, and which only needs to be developed along the right line. Our proper work with him is IMPROVEMENT, NOT TRANSFORMATION.

In view of this policy of the Government the light is dawning in the east for the Navajo, and he has a bright future. Being no longer guarded on the reservation, the great field of competitive labor is open before him. If, like Mahomet, the mountain does not come to him he goes to the mountain. If his crops fail him in seasons of drouth he goes forth with light heart and strong arm knowing that his labor is in demand as artisan and freighter or in the beet fields, or with the railroad construction crews, and that the honest laborer is ever worthy of his hire.

Appendix

The happiest man is he who learns from nature the lesson of worship.

Of that ineffable essence which we call Spirit, he that thinks most, will say least. We can foresee God in the coarse and, as it were, distant phenomena of matter; but when we try to define and describe himself, both language and thought desert us, and we are as helpless as fools and savages. The essence refuses to be recorded in propositions, but when man has worshiped him intellectually, the noblest ministry of nature is to stand as the apparition of God. It is the great organ through which the universal spirit speaks to the individual, and strives to lead the individual to it.

—EMERSON, *Essay on Nature.*

APPENDIX

Consisting of official letters and affidavits of government officials, both civil and military, relating to the Navajo Indians and their country, and to the causes which led to the Navajo war of 1861.

Also containing statements, from reliable sources, regarding the practice of the Mexicans capturing and holding Navajo Indians as slaves and servants.

AFFIDAVIT RELATING TO THE NAVAJO INDIANS AND THEIR COUNTRY

Santa Fe, New Mexico, July 3, 1865.
Brigadier General James H. Carleton sworn:
I am brigadier general of volunteers and major in the 6th regiment United States cavalry. I have been in the service twenty-five years. I first came to this Territory with General Sumner in 1851, and left in the fall of 1856. I returned again in the fall of 1862, and have been here ever since. I have been in command of this department since the 18th of September, 1862. My principal duties have been in connection with Indian affairs.

The Navajo country is a country of elevated *mesas*, destitute of water, and has some few ranges of mountains. Between these mesas are some low lands, whereon some springs and streams are found. These springs or streams are at great distance from each other, as compared with the frequency of water found elsewhere. These waters are of limited extent and volume; and the best of them sink in the earth at a short distance from their source. There are two exceptions to this general remark. One is the San Juan, a tributary of the Colorado of the West. Along this river are intervals of some extent, but separated from each other by ranges of mountains and *mesas* that abut upon the river. No one of these intervals is large enough for a reservation for one quarter of these Navajos. Formidable ranges of mountains are near by, in which they could hide, and no force of troops could keep them together. This is on the supposition that a reservation were selected on the San Juan river. Now, the cost of transportation of supplies from the Rio Grande to that point to subsist the Indians and to provide for the troops necessary to guard them in that locality would be immense, because the country to be traversed is difficult for the passage of wagons, and has long stretches through sage plains, without water in one or two instances of from forty to sixty miles.

The San Juan runs through a country bearing gold, which will soon attract miners to that region; and even if the Indians were placed there they would soon come into contact with that class of men, and great difficulties and complications would result therefrom.

The other exception to which I alluded is that of the Colorado Chiquito or Flax river. This is affluent to the Colorado of the West further down than the San Juan. It is subject to very great floods from the melting of snows on the Mogollon mountains at its source. When these floods have passed by, the river is very low, and its valleys become gradually covered with saline efflorescence, fatal to the growth of corn or wheat and the most of vegetables. Although this river runs through the old Navajo country, and these people have lived in its vicinity for ages, they themselves have never planted a field of

corn along its banks, which may be considered as
some evidence that it would not be a good place for a
reservation. The distance to the Colorado Chiquito
is nearly as great as to the San Juan, and the cost
of transportation as much.

I think the Navajo Indians are naturally as intelligent as any Indians I know of, including the
Pueblos. The Pueblo Indians are better informed
than the other Indians, from their long contact with
the influences of civilization and Christianity. The
Pueblos are Catholics. The Navajos are all pagans
with the exception of the Civollettanos. In Casten-
ada's narrative of the first expedition made into New
Mexico under Vasques de Coronada, in say 1543, 1544
and 1545, it is set forth that Indians were found in
pueblos as at the present day. Among these pueblos
doubtless Catholic missionaries established churches
and schools, and the Indians of those pueblos became
Christianized and partially civilized. This has raised
them very much above the nomadic Indians of the
country in point of intelligence and gentleness. With
the exception of one or two intervals of a few years
each, there has been a constant state of hostility between the people of New Mexico and the Navajo
Indians. Even in these intervals occasional forays
were made into the settlements to capture sheep and
cattle. The Mexicans would follow them into their
country to recapture the stolen stock, and would kill
some of the Indians and capture some of the women
and children and make slaves of them. But in times
when open hostilities existed these efforts were increased on each side to capture stock, women and
children, so that the country was kept in a continual
state of commotion. This was the state of things
when we acquired the territory from Mexico.

To the best of my recollection Colonel Doniphan,
who came here with General Kearney, made the first

expedition into the Navajo country in 1846. Colonel Washington made an expedition into their country in the year 1849; General Sumner in 1851. From 1851 until 1859 there was a period of comparative quiet, interrupted, as I have stated, by occasional forays, particularly on the part of the Navajos. In 1859 war again broke out, and in 1860 the Navajos attacked Fort Defiance. About this time Colonel Miles made an expedition into their country, and also Colonel Bonneville; and finally General Canby made a long campaign against them, leading his troops in person. When the Texan invasion of this country occurred, after General Canby's campaign against the Navajos, and when every soldier was employed to repel that invasion, then the Navajos, as well as the Apaches, rode over the country rough-shod. This was in the winter of 1861 and in the spring and summer of 1862. I relieved General Canby in command of the department; and this was the condition of the Navajos and Apaches at that time.

The Indian difficulties in New Mexico, since the treaty with Mexico, have obliged the United States to keep in that Territory a force whose average strength has been at least three thousand men, employes and all reckoned in. This covers a period of eighteen years. A large proportion of these troops have been cavalry, the most expensive arm in the military service, especially in New Mexico, where forage is very expensive. The horses required as remounts for this cavalry have to be brought across the plains from the States at great risk and expense. Sometimes large numbers have been stampeded en route and have never been heard from since. Many die before they reach this country. Those which arrive here it takes at least a year to acclimate; and after this the loss of horses by death, by being broken down, and lost on scouts, and killed in action, and stolen by Indians, is

A Navajo Weaver

enormous, compared with losses of cavalry horses in any other country. The same holds true of mules, more numerous necessarily than cavalry horses, by reason of the extent of country over which supplies have to be hauled to subsist and clothe the troops.

In this connection I feel constrained to say that much of the hostility manifested by many of the people of New Mexico against the reservation system, grows out of the fact that when this system goes into successful operation there will be no more tribes from which they can capture servants, and the military force being reduced to a very small number, the millions of dollars annually expended here on account of the military establishment will, in a great measure, cease.

The number of Indians, men, women and children, who have been captured or bought from the Utes, and who live in the families of the Territory, may be safely set down as at least three thousand. So far as my observation has gone, the Mexicans treat these Indians with great kindness. After a while they become conversant with the language, become attached to the families they live in, and very seldom care to run away. If they should attempt to run away I believe they would be captured by the owners. They are held as servants; as "hewers of wood and drawers of water." In my judgment three out of four of these servants are Navajos. These servants do not intermarry much with the Mexicans, but the women bear children from illicit intercourse. The offspring of this intercourse are considered as peons. The Indians upon the reservation, if properly cared for by the military commander, run no risk of being stolen or attacked.

CAUSES OF THE NAVAJO WARS

Slavery

Santa Fe, New Mexico, July 4, 1865.

Chief Justice Kirby Benedict sworn:

In August next I will have resided twelve years in New Mexico. I came here with the commission of judge, and have been a member of the supreme court and a judge of a district up to the present time; since in the summer of 1858 I have been chief justice. During the earlier part of this time the Navajo Indians kept peaceable relations with the United States government in this Territory and with the inhabitants. This condition of things was manifested a few days after my arrival, when a large deputation of the chiefs and principal men of the tribe came to Santa Fe and made a friendly visit to the governor, who was then also superintendent of Indian affairs in the Territory. A general friendship prevailed until an irritation occurred at Fort Defiance, from a negro having been killed at that place in a quarrel with an Indian who had come to the post. The negro is said to have been claimed as the slave of the commanding officer; satisfaction was required of the Navajos for the killing of the negro. I understand they offered to pay a sum, but the military exacted the delivering up of the Indian who had done the killing. Excuses were alleged, among others, that the Indian had fled beyond the tribe and their reach. The military remained unsatisfied, hostile feelings grew stronger and stronger on the part of the Navajos, and the former standing by their actions, the Navajos did acts of hostility directed firstly against the military, but which finally extended to and included the inhabitants of the Territory. Stealing, robberies and barbarities ensued, and the Indians, as a tribe, became involved, until the depredations upon life, security and property were so fre-

APPENDIX 107

quent and ruinous, a campaign was made against them under the command of Colonel Kit Carson, which was successful in bringing them to subjection, and causing a surrender as captives the principal portion of the tribe, men, women and children.

The Navajos were in the habit of making forays upon the ranches and settlements, stealing, robbing and killing and carrying away captives; the finding of herds and driving off sheep and other animals was carried on to a very ruinous extent; the killing of persons did not seem so much the object of their warfare as an incidental means of succeeding in other depredations. Sometimes, however, barbarous vengeance was exhibited and a thirst for blood. They carried away captives, but I can not now give any accurate idea of the number.

There are in the Territory a large number of Indians, principally females (women and children), who have been taken by force or stealth, or purchases, who have been among the various wild tribes of New Mexico or those adjoining. Of these a large proportion are Navajos. It is notorious that natives of this country have sometimes made captives of Navajo women and children when opportunities presented themselves; the custom has long existed here of buying Indian persons, especially women and children; the tribes themselves have carried on this kind of traffic. Destitute orphans are sometimes sold by their remote relations; poor parents also make traffic of their children. The Indian persons obtained in any of the modes mentioned are treated by those who claim to own them as their servants and slaves. They are bought and sold by and between the inhabitants at a price as much as is a horse or an ox. Those who buy, detain and use them seem to confide in the long-established custom and practice which prevails, and did prevail before this country was a portion of the United

States. Those who hold them are exceedingly sensitive of their supposed interest in them, and easily alarmed at any movements in the civil courts or otherwise to disposses them of their imagined property. The rich and those who have some quantities of property, are those chiefly who possess the persons I have mentioned; those usually have much popular influence in the country, and the exertion of this influence is one of the means by which they hope to retain their grasp upon their Indian slaves. The prices have lately ranged very high. A likely girl not more than eight years old, healthy and intelligent, would be held at a value of four hundred dollars or more. When they grow to womanhood they sometimes become mothers from the natives of the land, with or without marriage. Their children, however, by the custom of the country, are not regarded as property which may be bought and sold as have been their mothers. They grow up and are treated as having the rights of citizens. They marry and blend with the general population.

From my own observations I am not able to form an opinion satisfactory to my own mind of the number of Indians held as slaves or fixed domestic servants without their being the recipients of wages. Persons of high respectability for intelligence, who have made some calculations on the subject, estimate the number at various figures, from fifteen hundred to three thousand, and even exceeding the last number. The more prevalent opinion seems to be they considerably exceed two thousand.

As to federal officers holding this description of persons or trafficking in them, I can only say I see them attending the family of Governor Connelly, but whether claimed by himself, his wife, or both, I know not. I am informed the superintendent of Indian affairs has one in his family, but I can not state by what claim she is retained. From the social position occupied by the Indian agents, I presume all of them, except one, have the presence and assistance of the kind of persons mentioned; I cannot, however, state positively. In the spring of 1862, when Associate Justice Hubbell and myself conveyed our families to the States, he informed me at Las Vegas that he sold one Indian woman to a resident of that place preparatory to crossing the plains. I know of no law in this Territory by which property in a Navajo or other Indian can be recognized in any person whatever, any more than property can be recognized in the freest white man or black man. In 1855, while holding district court in the county of Valencia, a proceeding in habeas corpus was had before me on the part of a wealthy woman as petitioner, who claimed the possession and services of a Navajo girl then twelve years old, and who had been held by the petitioner near seven years. On the trial I held the girl to be a free person, and adjudged accordingly. In 1862 a proceeding in habeas corpus was instituted before me by an aged man who had held in service many years an Indian woman who had been, when a small child, bought from the Payweha Indians. The right of the master to the possession and services of the woman on the one side, and the right of the woman to her personal freedom, were put distinctly at issue. Upon the hearing I adjudged the woman to be a free woman; I held the claim of the master to be without foundation in law and against natural rights. In each of the cases the party adjudged against acquiesced in the decision, and no appeal was ever taken. In the examination of the cases it appeared that before the United States obtained New Mexico, captive and purchased Indians were held here by custom in the same manner they have been held since. The courts are open to them, but they are so influenced by the circumstances which surround them they do not seem to think of seeking the aid of the law to establish the enjoyment of their rights to freedom.

THE TROUBLE BETWEEN THE NAVAJOS AND THE SOLDIERS

Colonel Collins sworn:

I came to the Territory in the fall of 1827; I came as a merchant and trader. I traded back and forth from 1827 to 1843, making a trip once in three years. In 1843 I came and went into Old Mexico, and since then I have resided most of the time in Old and New Mexico; and since the war with Mexico I have resided in New Mexico all the time. I was superintendent of Indian affairs from 1847 until 1863, when I turned over the office to Dr. Steck.

About the commencement of June, a difficulty occurred between the Indians and the troops at Fort Defiance. That difficulty was occasioned by the Indians allowing their animals to run on lands which had been set apart by an arrangement with them as meadow lands for cutting hay for the post. Major Brooks was then in command of the post. The Indians were notified to keep their animals off. Finally, after they had been on the ground several times, a company of mounted men, under Captain McLane, of the rifles, was sent out, who ordered about seventy of the animals shot within the limits of the meadow. The result was, a very short time after this, a black boy, servant of Major Brooks, was killed by the Indians. The killing of the boy led to the war, which has continued up to this time.

After the killing of the boy a demand was made by Major Brooks on the principal men of the tribe for the delivery of the murderer, and were finally told that, unless he was given up, in thirty days war would be made on the tribe.

At this state of the case the facts were reported to General Garland, who was then in command of the department. General Garland, though not approving of the course which had been pursued, still thought proper not to recede from the demands which had been made, but thought proper to exact it. The result was an expedition against the Indians under Colonel Miles. My opinion was consulted, and I advised more specific means, and not to commence hostilities until every effort had been made to secure the murderer. An agent was sent out, in co-operation with the troops, to try and get the murderer and preserve the peace. He failed, the Indians refusing to deliver the murderer. The agent went with Captain McLane, with instructions to prevent hostilities until a council could be held with the chiefs, but on the way Captain McLane met some Indians and attacked them, getting wounded himself. Notwithstanding this attack, the Indians were collected and a council held, but it resulted in nothing, the Indians stating that they had no authority to deliver up the murderer, but offered to pay any price for the negro killed. The offer was refused, the troops insisting upon the delivery of the murderer. The consequence was open hostilities. The troops moved against the Indians in every direction, but they were not sufficiently damaged to bring them to terms.

After hostilities commenced, I insisted, with General Garland, that, as the war had been commenced, it should be prosecuted until the Indians sued for terms. General Garland concurred in this opinion, but was relieved about this time by Colonel Bonneville. Colonel Bonneville and myself concluded to go out and see the Indians at the expiration of the armistice, which would be about the 25th of December, at which time we concluded a treaty of peace with the Indians. My opinion was, that the war was improp-

erly commenced, and was improperly concluded by
not making the Indians comply with demand made
upon them.

The substance of the treaty was, that all stock
taken during hostilities should, as far as practicable,
be given up; and Colonel Bonneville agreed to enforce the condition on his part. The treaty was never
carried into effect, and in the summer of 1859 another
expedition was sent against the Indians, under Major
Simonson. He went out with instructions to enforce
that condition of the treaty to surrender the captured
stock. He failed to do so. That expedition was as
great a failure as the other. Hostilities continued. The
Indians continued their depredations, committing robberies and murders to a considerable extent, until
1860, when General Canby took command and made
an expedition against them. During this time the
Mexicans turned loose upon them, captured a good
many of their women and children.

General Canby made an expedition in 1860. He
was not very successful. He went into their country;
they asked for peace, and he made a treaty with them
and withdrew the troops. They, however, continued
their hostile depredations just about as before.

About that time the Rebellion broke out and the
Texans made their invasion. All the troops were with-
drawn from the Navajo country. The Navajos continued their depredations as usual, until General
Carleton came into the country, when he organized
his expedition, under Kit Carson, against them.

During the hostilities a band of friendly Indians
of about three hundred, increased by the addition of
those disposed to be friendly to about six hundred,
were greatly wronged, in my opinion, at Fort Wingate. There was some difficulty about a horse race.
The Indians, I think, won the race, and the Mexican
troops in the service refused to give up stakes, when a

Navajo Shepherds
(From the *Southern Workman*)

quarrel arose, and the troops fired into them; some were killed and some were wounded.

I cannot say that I could, but I was encouraged to think, but for the difficulty about the meadow lands and the killing of the negro boy of Major Brooks, I would have been able to maintain the peace with the Indians.

A NAVAJO SUPERSTITION LEADS TO THE KILLING OF NEGRO SLAVE

Dr. Louis Kennon sworn:

Am a resident of New Mexico; have been for twelve years last past; am a native of Georgia; am a physician by profession.

I think the Navajos have been the most abused people on the continent, and that in all hostilities the Mexicans have always taken the initiative with but one exception that I know of. When I first came here the Navajos were at peace, and had been for a long time. There was a pressure brought to bear upon the commander of the department by the Mexicans, and all Americans who pandered to that influence, to make war upon the Navajos. General Garland was commander of the Department at that time, and if you asked the Mexicans any reason for making war, they would give no other reason, but that the Navajos had a great many sheep and horses and a great many children. General Garland resisted their pressure until the unfortunate killing of a negro belonging to an officer at the post. The circumstances as I heard them are these:

Among the Navajos there is a great equality between the men and women; women own their own property independent of their husbands, and having property, are entitled to vote in the councils. They are also at liberty, if dissatisfied with their husbands, to leave them at will; but when they do so the husband asks to wipe out the disgrace by killing some one. A case of this kind occurred.

An Indian of a wealthy and influential family, had been deserted by his wife in this way, and he having had some real or imagined ill-treatment from this negro slave belonging to Major Brooks, of the 3rd Infantry, killed him. A demand was made for the surrender of the murderer, or war would follow. He was secreted by his family. The Indians killed some other Indian and brought in his body, insisting that it was the body of the murderer, killed while escaping from arrest. But the soldiers knew the murderer well, and they knew the folly of this pretense, so the demand was still insisted upon.

Meantime some Navajos near Albuquerque were murdered and robbed by Mexicans, and the Navajos made demand for the surrender of the murderers by General Garland. This was refused, and the surrender still insisted upon of the Indian who murdered the negro. The Indians offered to pay for the negro, but failed to surrender the murderer. War ensued, and there has been no permanent peace since. There have been intervals of quiet, but no substantial peace. Previous to the killing of the negro, the post had been in command of two very able and philanthropic gentlemen, Majors Kendricks and Backus, who kept the Navajos at peace by keeping the Mexicans away from them.

I was in the service of the United States as acting assistant surgeon, and was stationed at Fort Defiance in 1858, and was on a campaign against the Indians under Colonel Canby, and was in active service two months, scouting over the country, and therefore I know something about the country. In the old Navajo country the grazing facilities are inexhaustible. I saw no evidence of minerals; it is a red sandstone country, in which minerals do not exist.

I think the number of captive Navajo Indians held as slaves to be underestimated. I think there are from five to six thousand. I know of no family which can raise one hundred and fifty dollars but what purchases a Navajo slave, and many families own four or five — the trade in them being as regular as the trade in pigs or sheep. Previous to the war their price was from seventy-five to one hundred dollars; but now they are worth about four hundred dollars. But the other day some Mexican Indians from Chihuahua were for sale in Santa Fe. I have been conversant with the institution of slavery in Georgia, but the system is worse here, there being no obligation to care for the slave when he becomes old or worthless.

APPOINTMENT OF INDIAN AGENTS

Treatment of the Navajos by Mexicans

Major Griner sworn:

I first came to this Territory in 1851, staid until 1854, and then, again, in 1862, where I have remained since, with the exception of the time of the Texan invasion. I came here first as Indian agent, and was at first assigned to duty at Taos, as agent for the Apaches and Utes, but afterwards acted as general superintendent under Governor Calhoun, and travelled over pretty much all the Territory. I was Indian agent from 1851 until 1853, being then appointed secretary.

The great difficulty in our Indian policy is in the selection of Indian agents, who are generally appointed for political services. Mr. Wingfield came here as an agent because he was the friend of Mr. Dawson of Georgia; Mr. Wolly, an old man of seventy years of age, because he was the friend of Mr. Clay; Mr.

Weightman, because he wished to be returned as delegate; and myself, because I could sing a good political song. Neither of us was by habit or education better fitted to be Indian agent than to follow any other business. The general policy of selecting men as agents for political services, rather than fitness for the position, and frequently changing them, is a great cause of all our Indian difficulties, in my opinion. I was changed just as I was about to be of service, and had become acquainted with the Indians, and had acquired their confidence, and could get them to do as I desired.

When I left here I went away with a high opinion of the system adopted by the Spaniards — I mean the pueblos, which are reservations. I look upon them as models, and their government as models for Indians. Their governments are entirely democratic; they select their own officers and administer their own laws. At first they had no farms, and depended on their own industry for subsistence, and none have ever been found guilty of a criminal offense. The only difficulty in our government doing as the Spaniards did is on account of religion. The Spaniards planted a church in the center of each pueblo, the priest naming the babies and baptizing them; and the priest was in fact the agent of the Spanish government, and had charge of the temporal as well as the spiritual affairs. This of course would be impracticable under our government.

In my experience I have never known a serious difficulty in the Territory between the Indians and citizens which did not originate mainly with the latter. One of the first exciting difficulties in the Territory arose from the capture of Mrs. White, a very beautiful woman, and her little daughter, by the Jicarilla Apaches. I was appointed to investigate it. I found that at Las Vegas the troops had, without any sufficient cause or provocation, fired upon the Indians, and they in revenge joined with some Utes and attacked the next train coming from the States, killing Mr. White and others, and capturing his wife and child; and also the stage, with ten passengers, was taken and all killed. A war was the consequence.

Another instance on the part of Mangus Colorado, the chief of the Apaches: During my administration as acting superintendent of Indian affairs I was present with General Sumner to make a treaty of peace. He was an Indian of remarkable intelligence and great character. I asked him the cause of the difficulties with the people in Chihuahua and Sonora, for at that time, under the treaty with Mexico, we were bound to protect its people from the attacks of the Indians residing in New Mexico. He said: "I will tell you. Sometime ago my people were invited to a feast; *aguardiente*, or whiskey, was there; my people drank and became intoxicated, and were lying asleep, when a party of Mexicans came in and beat out their brains with clubs. At another time a trader was sent among us from Chihuahua. While innocently engaged in trading, often leading to words of anger, a cannon concealed behind the goods was fired upon my people and quite a number were killed. Since that Chihuahua has offered a reward for our scalps, $150 each, and we have been hunted down ever since"; and, with great emphasis and in the most impressive manner, he added, "How can we make peace with such people?"

I have also since learned from the agent of the tribe, Dr. Steck, that sixty Indians of the same tribe were poisoned by strychnine. The whole country of Sonora and Chihuahua has been devastated by these Indians. This same chief was afterwards taken prisoner by our own troops and confined in the guard house, and was killed while so confined by the sentinel.

The Navajos, while Mr. Dodge was their agent and Major Kendrick and Major Backus in command of the posts in their country, were friendly and peaceable, owing to the prudence and wisdom with which those officers discharged the duties of their stations, and, in my opinion, had they remained, or persons of equal prudence, there would not have been any hostilities on the part of the Navajos. There was a change of agents and military commanders in their country, and a war broke out in the consequence of the killing of a negro boy of Major Brooks', as I am informed. Another cause of trouble has been in consequence of the capture of their flocks and herds, and their women and children for servants.

About a year ago a Navajo travelling with his wife and two or three children was shot down by a company of Mexican troops. He defended himself bravely to the last, but he was killed and scalped — one of the party giving me an account of it, saying his bravery won their admiration. He brought me the scalp, which I now present to the committee.

PLANS OF THE MILITARY TO SUBJUGATE THE NAVAJOS

Headquarters Department of New Mexico,
Santa Fé, New Mexico,
September 30, 1862.

General:

I have the honor to inform you that I relieved General Canby in the command of this department on the 18th instant, and he left this city for Washington, D. C., four days afterwards. I find that during the raid which was made into this Territory by some armed men from Texas, under Brigadier General Sibley, of the army of the so-called Confederate States, the Indians, aware that the attention of our troops could not, for the time, be turned toward them, commenced robbing the inhabitants of their stock, and killed, in various places, a great number of people; the Navajos on the western side, and the Mescalero Apaches on the eastern side of the settlements both committing these outrages at the same time, and during the last year that has passed have left the people greatly impoverished. Many farms and settlements near Fort Stanton have been entirely abandoned.

To punish and control the Mescaleros, I have ordered Fort Stanton to be reoccupied. That post is in the heart of their country, and hitherto when troops occupied it those Indians were at peace. I have sent Colonel Christopher Carson (Kit Carson) with five companies of his regiment of New Mexican volunteers, to Fort Stanton. One of these companies, on foot, will hold the post and guard the stores, while four companies mounted, under Carson, will operate against the Indians until they have been punished for their recent aggressions. The lieutenant colonel, with four companies of the same regiment, will move into the Navajo country and establish and garrison a post on the Gallo, which was selected by General Canby; it is called Fort Wingate. I shall endeavor to have this force, assisted by some militia which have been called out by the governor of the Territory, perform such services among the Navajos as will bring them to feel that they have been doing wrong.

I am, general, very respectfully, your obedient servant   JAMES H. CARLETON,
Brigadier General Commanding.

Brigadier General Lorenzo Thomas,
  Adjutant General, U. S. A.,
  Washington, D. C.

KIT CARSON INVADES THE NAVAJOS' STRONGHOLD AND
CAPTURES MANY PRISONERS

Headquarters Department of New Mexico,
Las Cruces, New Mexico,
February 7, 1864.

General:

I have the honor herewith to inclose a copy of the report of Colonel Christopher Carson, commanding the expedition against the Navajo Indians, of his success in marching a command through the celebrated *Canyon de Chelly*, the great stronghold of that tribe, and of the killing of twenty-three of the warriors and the capture of a large number of prisoners. These prisoners are now en route to the Bosque Redondo.

* * * * * * *

This is the first time any troops, whether when the country belonged to Mexico or since we acquired it, have been able to pass through the Canyon de Chelly, which, for its great depth, its length, its perpendicular walls, and its labyrinthine character, has been regarded by eminent geologists as the most remarkable of any "fissure" (for such it is held to be) upon the face of the globe. It has been the great fortress of the tribe since time out of mind. To this point they fled when pressed by our troops. Colonel Washington, Colonel Sumner, and many other commanders have made an attempt to go through it, but had to retrace their steps. It was reserved for Colonel Carson to be the first to succeed; and I respectfully request the government will favorably notice that officer, and give him a substantial reward for this crowning act in a long life spent in various capacities

Crossing the Desert
(From the *Southern Workman*)

in the service of his country in fighting the savages among the fastnesses of the Rocky Mountains.

* * * * * * *

I believe this will be the last Navajo war. The persistent efforts which have been and will continue to be made can hardly fail to bring in the whole tribe before the year ends. I beg respectfully to call the serious attention of the government to the destitute condition of the captives, and beg for authority to provide clothing for the women and children. Every preparation will be made to plant large crops for their subsistence at the Bosque Redondo the coming spring. Whether the Indian department will do anything for these Indians or not you will know. But whatever is to be done should be done at once. At all events, as I before wrote you, *"we can feed them cheaper than we can fight them."*

I am, general, very respectfully,
Your obedient servant,
JAMES H. CARLETON,
Brigadier General, Commanding.

Brigadier General Lorenzo Thomas,
Adjutant General U. S. A.,
Washington, D. C.

KIT CARSON RECEIVES HONORABLE MENTION FOR SUB-
DUING THE NAVAJOS

Headquarters Department of New Mexico,
Santa Fé, N. M., February 27, 1864.

General:

What with the Navajos I have captured and those who have surrendered we have now over three thousand, and will, without doubt, soon have the whole tribe. I do not believe they number now much over five thousand, all told. You have doubtless seen the last of the Navajo war — a war that has been continued with but few intermissions for one hundred and eighty years, and which, during that time, has been marked by every shade of atrocity, brutality and ferocity which can be imagined or which can be found in the annals of conflict between our own and the aboriginal race.

I beg to congratulate you and the country at large on the prospect that this formidable band of robbers and murderers have at last been made to succumb. To Colonel Christopher Carson, first cavalry New Mexico volunteers, Capt. Asa B. Casey, United States Army, and the officers and men who served in the Navajo campaign, the credit for these successes is mainly due. * * * * * *

I am, general, very respectfully,

Your obedient servant,

JAMES H. CARLETON,

Brigadier General, Commanding.

Brigadier General Lorenzo Thomas,

Adjutant General U. S. A.,

Washington, D. C.

REPORT OF THE CONDITION OF THE NAVAJO PRISONERS
OF WAR AT THE BASQUE REDONDO, NEW MEXICO

Headquarters Department of New Mexico,

Santa Fé, N. M., March 12, 1864.

General:

Since writing to you on the 6th instant in relation to the Navajo Indians, I have been informed that there are now three thousand of them — men, women and children — who have surrendered at Fort Canby, and are about starting for the Bosque Redondo. These, with those now at that place and enroute thither, will make five thousand five hundred, without including the captive Mescalero Apaches. There will doubtless be more Navajos come into Fort Canby — what are known as the *Ricos* of the tribe — men who have stock, and will doubtless be able to subsist themselves upon that stock until we are better prepared to take care of them. Colonel Carson has been instructed to send in the poor and destitute first. The Ricos will come in afterwards. Among the poor are nearly or quite all the ladrones and murderers, so that we have already in our hands the bad men of the tribe. An exact census will be taken of the Ricos, and a statement made of the probable amount of their stock, which has hitherto been greatly exaggerated, in my opinion. When this is done, Colonel Carson will himself come in from the Navajo country and go down to the Bosque Redondo to give the Indians the counsel they so much need just at this time as to how to start their farms and to commence their new mode of life. You have from time to time been informed of every step which I have taken with reference to operations against Indians in this country. I multiplied, as much as possible, the points of contact between our forces and themselves, and, although no great battle has been fought, still the persistent efforts of small parties acting simultaneously over a large extent of country, have destroyed a great many and harrassed the survivors until they have become thoroughly subdued. Now, when they have surrendered and are at our mercy, they must be taken care of — must be fed, clothed and instructed. This admits neither of discussion nor delay. These six thousand mouths must eat, and these six thousand bodies must be clothed. When it is considered what a magnificent pastoral and mineral country they have surrendered — a country whose value can hardly be estimated — the mere pittance, in comparison, which must at once be given to support them, sinks into insignificance as a price for their natural heritage.

They must have two million pounds of bread-stuffs sent from the States. This can be done by installments — the first installment to be started at once; say five hundred thousand pounds of flour and corn, in equal parts. The next installment to reach the Bosque in August next, and all to be delivered by the middle of next November. This amount will last them, with what we can buy here, until the crops come off in 1865; when from that time forward, so far as food may go, they will, in my opinion, be self-sustaining.

Add to these breadstuffs four thousand head of cattle, to come by installments of five hundred each — the first to reach the Bosque by the first of July next, and all to be there by the middle of November. Salt can be bought here, but you can not buy the breadstuffs or the meat; they are not in the country, and consequently can not be got at any price. In view of the contingencies of delays, accidents, etc., I have put all the troops on half rations, and, at most of the posts, ordered that no grain be issued to cavalry horses. These six thousand people must be fed until you can get us relieved by sending supplies, as above named, from the States. This matter, being of paramount importance, is alluded to here as the first which will claim your attention or, rather, your action; for the matter is imperative — is self evident; it needs no deliberation, as you will see, and admits of no delay.

Next comes the wherewithal to clothe these poor women and these little children. You will find in a duplicate of the letter which I wrote to you on the 6th of March, and which is herewith inclosed, a list of such articles as are absolutely needed now.

Then come agricultural implements, which must be here to insure the crops. Then the tools, cooking utensils, etc., etc., lists of which you will also find enveloped with this letter.

I beg to call your attention to the most important consideration — the management of the Navajos upon the reservation. The amount of ability and business habits and tact necessary in one who should be selected to direct these people in their work, and in the systematic employment of their seasons of labor — in one having forecast to see their coming wants and necessities, and having resources of practical sense to provide for those wants and necessities — in one who would have the expending of the funds which must be appropriated for their support — cannot be commanded for the sum of fifteen hundred dollars per annum, given to an Indian agent. The law to be framed granting an annuity to the tribe should also provide for a *supervisor*, with a salary at least of three thousand dollars a year, and an *assistant supervisor*, with a salary equal to that of an Indian agent. These men should be selected with great care. The assistant supervisor should be apt at accounts — practical as a man of business — of resources as a farmer and as a mechanic — of patience, industry and temperance — one whose heart would be in his business, and who would himself believe that his time belonged to the government, and need not be spent mainly in "grinding axes" elsewhere at the expense of the United States. The superintendent need have, and should have, no further control than simply to audit the accounts.

If all this be set forth in the law, so far as salary and duties go, the whole plan will go into successful operation at once. If not set forth in the law, you may depend upon it, general, that, with the changes in superintendents — with diverse counsels and diverse interests, and lack of fixedness of purpose and system — the Indians will not be properly cared for, and, in room of becoming a happy, prosperous and contented people, will become sad and desponding, and will soon lapse into idle and intemperate habits. You wish them to become a people whom all can contemplate with pride and satisfaction as *proteges* of the United States — a people who, in return for having given you their country, have been remembered and carefully provided for by a powerful Christian nation like ourselves. But unless you make in the law all the arrangements here contemplated, you will find this interesting and intelligent race of Indians will fast diminish in numbers, until, within a few years only, not one of those who boasted in the proud name of Navajo will be left to upbraid us for having taken their birthright, and then left them to perish.

With other tribes whose lands we have acquired, ever since the Pilgrims stepped on shore at Plymouth, this has been done too often. For pity's sake, if not moved by any other consideration, let us, as a great nation, for once treat the Indian as he deserves to be treated. It is due to ourselves as well as to them, that this be done.

Having this purpose in view, I am sure the lawmakers will not be ungenerous; nor will they be unmindful of all those essential points which, in changing a people from a nomadic to an agricultural condition of life, should be kept in view, in order to guard them against imposition, to protect them in their rights, to encourage them in their labors, and to provide for all their reasonable wants.

The exodus of this whole people from the land of their fathers is not only an interesting but a touching sight. They have fought us gallantly for years on years; they have defended their mountains and their stupendous canyons with a heroism which any people might be proud to emulate; but when, at length, they found it was their destiny too, as it had been that of their brethren, tribe after tribe, away back toward the rising of the sun, to give way to the insatiable progress of our race, they threw down their arms, and, as brave men entitled to our admiration and respect, have come to us with confidence in our magnanimity, and feeling that we are too powerful and too just a people to repay that confidence with meanness or neglect — feeling that for having sacrificed to us their beautiful country, their homes, the associations of their lives, the scenes rendered classic in their traditions, we will not dole out to them a miser's pittance in return for what we know to be a princely realm.

This is a matter of such vital importance that I can not intrust to the accidents of a mail, but transmit this letter and its accompanying papers by a special messenger — Colonel James L. Collins, late superintendent of Indian affairs — who can be consulted with profit not only by the War and Interior Departments, but by the proper committees in Congress, whose attention will have to be called at once to the subject.

*   *   *   *   *   *   *

I am, general, very respectfully,
Your obedient servant,
JAMES H. CARLETON,
Brigadier General, Commanding.

Brigadier General Lorenzo Thomas,
    Adjutant General U. S. A.,
      Washington, D. C.

Report of the United States Indian Agent on the Condition of the Navajo Indians

United States Indian Service,
Navajo Agency, N. Mex., August 12, 1889.

Sir:

If not an impossibility, it is at least a very difficult matter, to obtain a full and correct census of the tribe. Twenty years ago when the Government returned them to the reservation from their banishment to Texas, they numbered from 12,000 to 13,000 in addition to which there were nearly 400 who were never captured and who remained in the mountains until the return of their brethren. Since then the population has increased at a moderate rate, and from the most reliable information obtainable I should judge it is now in the neighborhood of 21,000. This number is divided into ten clans, each of which has a chief, as follows:

CLAN	CHIEF
Man That Went Around	White Head
Black Sheep	Son of His Father
Close to Streams	Balgoonda
Big Water	Gano Muncho and Manuelito
Bitter Water	Be-tchi-bnu
Meeting the Water	Sandoval
Blackwood	Sin-in-is-Ky
Leaves	Long Back
Red Bank	Mariana
Band That Escaped	Loud Man

The principal wealth of the Navajos is their stock, which, like the population, it is a difficult matter to

A Navajo Athlete

estimate, but from the most reliable information at hand I should say is about as follows:

Horses 250,000
Mules   500
Burros 1,000
Cattle 5,000
Sheep 700,000
Goats 200,000

By common consent the sheep are considered the property of the women, and are clipped in the spring and fall each year. In the past twelve months I should judge the crop to be about 2,100,000 pounds. Of this the seven traders on the reservation have purchased more than they did a year ago, but by far the greater portion of it has been marketed with the thirty-odd traders who surround the reservation at different points, and with stores on the railroad at points from twelve to twenty miles from the reservation.

In addition to his stock the Indian counts his wealth by his beads and silver ornaments. The only money known to him is silver coin. After supplying his wants of food and clothing his surplus cash is converted into ornaments by native workmen, which are worn on the body or used on trappings for his horses. When he becomes hard up, between harvests, which is by no means uncommon, these ornaments are pawned with the traders, but are invariably redeemed.

The Navajo has always been taught to estimate his wealth by the number of horses he owns, and there are many who own hundreds of heads each, while a few count their possessions by thousands. As these animals do not command good prices off the reservation, and as they are rapidly increasing in numbers, the Indian is beginning to look about for a

means of increasing his wealth in other shape. Quite
a number of them are turning their attention to cattle
raising and are trading their horses for calves wherever they can do so. In this I encourage them whenever the opportunity presents itself, because cattle
are as easily raised as horses and a market can always
be found for them at fair cash prices.

The reservation contains nearly 2,250,000* acres,
which for picturesque grandeur can not be excelled
in the United States, but considered as a farming
country would require an elastic imagination to produce a favorable comment. The altitude of the country ranges from 5,000 to 7,500 feet above sea level and
is never favored with rain at a season of the year
when growing grain can derive any benefit from it.
Where there is any soil it is sandy, but produces
well when water can be had for irrigation. I do not
suppose there are over 50,000 acres of tillable soil on
the reservation, although the mountains in many
places furnish ample pasture for stock. In the past
year the Indians have cultivated about 8,000 acres.
Their crops are looking well, particularly wheat, and
promise a good harvest. In the past year, the Department furnished me for distribution among the
tribe fifty bushels of wheat, some potatoes, and a
small assortment of garden seeds. The supply was
soon exhausted and fell far short of meeting the
demand. Owing to the abundance of snow which
falls here in the winter and the dry weather which
follows in the spring, it is my opinion that winter
wheat can be successfully grown on the reservation,
and I will ask that a sufficient quantity for seeding
be furnished this season.

I am informed that last year the Department
spent $12,000 on the construction of irrigation ditches

_____

*Now 9,503,763 acres.

on the reservation. I have been over the ground where the work was done, and am sorry to say that it amounts to nothing. The ditches were evidently built without any regard to utility, durability, or knowledge of the subject. In many places the alleged ditch was merely a furrow turned with a plow. No care was ever taken of them, and even if they had been constructed in a workmanlike manner they would have been useless this year, as the Indians of their own accord will take no care of them, and from this cause the crop last year was a failure. Where irrigation is undertaken in a sensible manner there is no reason why the crops should fail. There are many valleys on the reservation where storage reservoirs could be constructed which would hold a sufficient quantity of water to thoroughly irrigate all the tillable land in the neighborhood. As the Indian will not keep ditches in repair, the reservation should be divided into four districts for irrigation purposes and each should be placed in charge of a competent farmer, whose duty it would be to see that all the ditches and laterals are kept in good repair, and at the same time assist and instruct the Indians in farming. Until some such plan as this is adopted and followed, irrigation by the Indians will be a failure. If it is adopted and followed the Indians will soon learn to take care of themselves, and in a few years will become independent of any assistance or information from the whites. In this connection it is proper to state that Lieut. J. M. Stotzenburg, of the Sixth Cavalry, is now engaged in making a survey of the reservation for irrigating purposes, and will submit a report in a short time.

On the first of February last nearly a third of the tribe were off the reservation, many of them being scattered along the line of the railroad, and very few of them doing any good for themselves or others. Since that time about 150 families have been induced to return and resume their residence, where they properly belong and where every Navajo should be. It will doubtless take some time to get them all back, but if a time is specified in which to do the work, I anticipate no trouble in bringing about the desired end.

The influence of the chiefs is rapidly waning and has almost disappeared. It is very seldom their advice is sought — never in matters of general importance — and when offered it is rarely accepted. When disputes occur which cannot be settled among themselves, the matter is generally laid before the agent, whose decision and advice are accepted in good faith by the interested parties. But I am sorry to say the medicine men still exert a bad influence over the members of the tribe, although they are losing ground and many come in to consult the agency physician. Like many other tribes the Navajos are, unfortunately, the victims of that loathsome disease, syphilis, and being transmissable from one generation to another, it is constantly becoming more widespread. It is a source of much regret that present facilities render it utterly impossible to eradicate this fearful malady and the many ills resulting therefrom. A hospital at the agency, where protracted treatment could be enforced, offers the only hope of permanent relief, as the Indian cannot be relied upon to persevere in the protracted use of remedies. It is confidently believed that with the proper facility for eliminating this contaminating and fatal disease, the sanitary condition of these hardy people could be brought almost to perfection, as nine-tenths of all their numerous complaints are traceable thereto.

Another matter to which I wish to call the attention of the Department is the need of an industrial school here at which the older boys can be taught trades. They are all willing to learn, and, in making improvements or repairs at the agency, display an aptitude which is at once surprising and gratifying. It may be urged against the teaching of such branches here that the government has made ample provisions for such instruction at other schools to which these children may be sent. Granted. But on the other hand there are many reasons why such a school should be established here. By reference to statistics I find that the Navajos represent nearly one-twelfth of the entire Indian population of the United States, though in reality I believe one-tenth would be nearer correct, and they are steadily increasing in population. In point of numbers, then, the reservation would support such a school. The government has sent a sawmill here to cut lumber for the Indians with which they may build houses. All who can avail themselves of the benefits to be derived from it wish to do so, and daily I have applications for materials and tools. None of these Indians are carpenters, and must of course labor under great disadvantages in building unless they bring to their assistance white labor, which is very expensive in this locality. Of course, under such circumstances, they all fully appreciate the benefits to be derived from the knowledge of the trades and want their children to learn one. There are a number of the boys who want to learn to be tinners. Some want to be wagonmakers; some blacksmiths, and the proportions of the school at present would warrant the establishment of a tailor shop and shoemaker shop. The school quarters, which were built to accommodate sixty pupils, are now crowded to overflowing with ninety-nine pupils from all portions of the reservation, and representing the most thrifty and enterprising families among the Navajos.

Nothing will induce the Navajo to send his children away from the reservation to attend school. His affection for his offspring is equal to that of any race of people on the face of the earth. He visits his children at the school frequently, and when he does not reside too far away, likes to take them home with him occasionally for a day or two for recreation. He wants them near him, so that he can go and see them at any time. In case of sickness of a child at school it is remarkable how quickly his parents find it out, and come to see him, or should a parent be taken sick at home the children are immediately sent after. The Navajo is also very superstitious, which will not allow him to send his children off the reservation to school. Some years ago, Manuelito, the famous war chief of the tribe, lost two sons by death while attending school in the East, and since then no Navajo will listen to a proposition to send a child of his to an Eastern school.

But aside from these reasons I think it better that the industrial branches be taught at home where their parents can see them at work and witness the advantages to be derived from such an education. These Indians are close observers, and take much more interest in work done by their own people than when it is manufactured by the whites. Send an Indian East to educate him for the benefit of his tribe, and should he take a notion to remain among the whites, as was the case in the only instance under my observation here, it is a discouragement to the Department in its efforts to benefit the red man, inasmuch as it works no good to the Indians, but on the contrary causes them to prefer the company of their sons at home in ignorance rather than risk sending them away for an education with the chance of never seeing them again.

Polygamy is still practiced on the reservation, but to a very limited extent, and is discouraged as much as possible. The Navajos are fond of gambling. Some of them follow it for a living, and most of them are willing to engage in it whenever an opportunity offers. When a crowd of them met at the agency it was the custom to spread a blanket anywhere and indulge their favorite proclivity. This led to petty thieving in several cases, which I promptly punished and broke up the indulgence in this locality. This is the sum total of the sins of 21,000 ignorant and un-civilized American Indians as has been reported to me in a little over five months, and the Navajos invariably report the wrong doings of their neighbors. Can any community of like numbers in the civilized world make as good a showing?

It has been reported that rich mineral ores, particularly silver, abound on certain portions of the reservation and would likely cause trouble between the Indians and adventurous prospectors. In the latter part of March it was reported to me that a band of miners and cow-boys was being organized at Gallup, New Mexico, for the purpose of invading the reservation in search of mineral. The report proved to be correct, but, after a talk with the leaders, I persuaded them to desist, and the expedition was abandoned. I am informed that several have lost their lives in adventurous search for this mythical wealth, and it is not surprising. The mountains which are said to contain this alleged wealth are the Navajos' place of worship. When they are sick they go there to effect a cure, and it is their belief that if they are invaded by the white man they will die. Add to this the fact that the white man has no business there, and it is not surprising that he finds it exceedingly dangerous. I have investigated all these stories of mineral wealth as thoroughly as circumstances would permit, and find there is nothing in them. Mineral does not exist on the reservation, but if it was in paying quantities the Indian would not be slow to avail himself of it.

Aside from the regular Sabbath exercises in the school by the superintendent, the Navajos are without religious instruction, and do not seem to be considered fit subjects for missionary work by any of the great religious denominations of the world. Still these Indians are religiously inclined, and all their ceremonies are religious in character, though not of the orthodox requirements.   While remembering in a substantial way the heathen of other lands and warmer climes, the Navajo of the United States should not be entirely blotted from memory.

Very respectfully,
Your obedient servant,
C. E. VANDEVER,
United States Indian Agent.
The Commissioner of Indian Affairs.

AUTHOR'S NOTE:—There are now in the Navajo country Missions maintained by the Methodists, Baptists, Episcopalians, Catholics, Presbyterians and Dutch Reform churches.

1486155R0

Printed in Great Britain by
Amazon.co.uk, Ltd.,
Marston Gate.